Essential Moon Astrology

Essential Moon Astrology

How to gain insight from the Moon for a deeper understanding of yourself, your relationships, and daily life

Joanna Watters

CICO BOOKS

This book is dedicated to my New Moon niece Sara, with love and admiration for keeping the flag of the creative life flying.

Published in 2026 by CICO Books
An imprint of Ryland Peters & Small Ltd
20–21 Jockey's Fields
London WC1R 4BW
www.rylandpeters.com
Email: euregulations@rylandpeters.com

10 9 8 7 6 5 4 3 2 1

A CIP record for this book is available from the British Library.
US Library of Congress CIP data has been applied for.

ISBN: 978-1-80065-594-2

Printed in China

Illustrator: Eleanor Carter
Commissioning editor: Kristine Pidkameny
Desk editors: Imogen Valler-Miles and Stephanie Durrant
Senior designer: Emily Breen
Art director: Sally Powell
Production manager: Gordana Simakovic
Publishing manager: Carmel Edmonds

The authorised representative in the EEA is
Authorised Rep Compliance Ltd.,
Ground Floor. 71 Lower Baggot Street,
Dublin, D01 P593, Ireland
www.arccompliance.com

FSC
www.fsc.org
MIX
Paper | Supporting responsible forestry
FSC® C106563

Contents

Introduction

Astrology has been around for a very, very long time, dating back to the third millennium BCE. In our own times, we live with a form of astrology that has been kept alive through newspaper and magazine columns, and the birthday card industry. We all know our Sun sign in the same way that we know our date of birth.

Intriguingly, from the evidence of markings on bones and cave walls, we learn that the lunar cycle was being noted as early as 25,000 years ago. When we move beyond media astrology, and venture into the world of horoscopy, we find that the Sun and the Moon carry equal symbolic weight and work together as a pair. Together they're known as the Lights or the Luminaries—they're the source of our light by night or day, and they symbolize the essence of life itself.

At a physical level, we take the Sun for granted. He is our life force, part of everyone's world, and we all share the wonder at the glorious beauty of sunrises and sunsets. The attendant symbolism of life–death–rebirth works its way into our understanding from the moment our consciousness starts to evolve, through to the final chapter of our twilight years.

The Moon is also part of everyone's world and yet, from childhood, we know she is different. We can't look at the Sun, and in that respect the Sun is ignored. It is only in the glory and darkness of the night sky that we can connect with the heavens, the beauty and brightness of Venus and Jupiter, the glitter of red that is Mars, and the knowing that other planets are too distant to be seen by the naked eye.

It is the Moon who dominates our skies from very early on in our lives. As children, we draw pictures of "the man in the Moon," that large, round, smiley face twinkling down on us. Of all the heavenly bodies above us, it is only at the unmissable Moon that we gaze. Month in, month out, we can watch the lunar cycle, seeing with our own eyes her constantly changing face, from the monthly first sliver of silver to the swelling of fullness. We grow up with the brief but bright guiding light of the Full Moon, and

we learn to make a wish as soon as we see the glimmering crescent. Thus it is the Moon who awakens our first sense of something magical, and our first awareness that we live in a vast, mysterious, yet highly organized universe.

Remember that you come into this world with a horoscope in the same way that you arrive with your fingerprints and the color of your hair. It is your celestial DNA and you can't be separated from it. You are your chart, your chart is you—same thing. Your horoscope is based on the exact date, place, and time of your birth. Think of this as a photograph snapped at the moment of birth, a picture of the heavens that captures the exact position of all of the planets as seen from a precise location on planet Earth. In terms of natal astrology, everything starts with this frozen moment in time. In that moment, we find where all our "natal" planets are in our horoscope.

Getting to know our Moon sign, or natal Moon, and becoming familiar with it in the same way that we recognize our Sun sign characteristics, is one of astrology's greatest gifts. In Chapter 1, the description of the zodiac signs as expressed through the Moon will connect you with your emotional nature, regardless of your Sun sign. Here we enter the lunar world of needs, early conditioning, and often unconscious responses. In this respect, it is easy to see how the Moon is a vital consideration in personal relationships.

Move over the love planets Venus and Mars. It is the Moon sign that holds the silver keys to true caring, compatibility, and the satisfying sharing of daily life. You can find out how to look up your natal Moon on page 140.

Beyond our emotional makeup and relationships, the Moon's daily journey continually and accurately mirrors our own. Chapter 2 covers how we can simply observe or consciously harness the lunar symbolism as the Moon works her way through the 12 signs each month. The more familiar we become with this kind of astrology, the more we recognize and become aware of the symbolism of the signs at work, and the more we can venture into the world of prediction.

We are steeped in lunar symbolism and timing, almost without realizing it, as explored in Chapter 3, which looks at lunations (New and Full Moons) and Eclipses. Finally, in Chapter 4, you can read about the Moon's unique role in the progressed chart, highlighting the nature of a life event as well as pinpointing timing, and also about the phenomenon of the Lunar Return that adds another arrow to the astrologer's interpretative and predictive bow.

The Moon is essential. Without her, the world of astrology would be a far less detailed and intricate place. Whatever the bigger picture, it is the Moon who so often has the last word. Enjoy your voyage of lunar discovery.

Astrology Basics

All chart interpretation work starts with the building blocks of craft. This is the part of astrology that we can all learn by heart, arming ourselves with the unchanging information of the nature of the signs, planetary symbolism, the elements and modes, and the meaning of the Houses. From these basics, every horoscope is born.

What is the Zodiac?

All astrology starts with 12 signs of the zodiac, the Sun signs. Based on the position of the Sun at the time of your birth, the Sun sign symbolizes our essential self, the core of our personality, and purpose around which everything else revolves. The horoscope shows us that we are all, in fact, a mixture of signs, but the Sun sign is nevertheless always a central consideration.

The chart below shows the 12 Sun signs, including their symbols, dates, and key characteristics associated with each sign.

12 Sun Signs with Their Symbols and Dates

Aries March 21 – April 19
Immediate, incisive, direct, innovative, inspirational, effective

Taurus April 20 – May 20
Stoical, reliable, sensuous, appetitive, tolerant, risk averse

Gemini May 21 – June 20
Multitasking, animated, talkative, inventive, resourceful, mischievous

Cancer June 21 – July 22
Indirect, cautious, evasive, sympathetic, instinctive, tenacious

Leo July 23 – August 22
Creative, proud, warm, self-reliant, efficient, assured

Virgo August 23 – September 22
Fastidious, analytical, diligent, dutiful, quirky, astute

Libra September 23 – October 22
Sociable, charming, indecisive, diplomatic, discursive, fair

Scorpio October 23 – November 21
Determined, forceful, thorough, intense, passionate, resourceful

Sagittarius November 22 – December 21
Intuitive, spontaneous, optimistic, friendly, enthusiastic, ethical

Capricorn December 22 – January 19
Reserved, serious, industrious, focused, pragmatic, courteous

Aquarius January 20 – February 18
Systematic, impartial, inquisitive, friendly, humane, original

Pisces February 19 – March 20
Sensitive, empathic, artistic, addictive, instinctive, visionary

The Planets and the Signs

The first seven heavenly bodies—the Sun, the Moon, Mercury, Venus, Mars, Jupiter, and Saturn—are known as the "personal" planets. They are followed by the outer, much slower-moving planets of Uranus, Neptune, and Pluto. Modern-day astrology now also includes the minor planet Chiron, which was discovered in 1977.

Each planet travels through the 12 signs of the zodiac (Aries through Pisces), but at a different speed. The Moon takes just 29 days, the other "personal" planets take from between a year (such as the Sun) to nearly 30 years, whereas the cycles of the outer planets are significantly slower. All the planets in a horoscope have their own symbolic nature.

The Symbolism of the Planets

Sun Our essential self, consciousness, the core of our personality, the purpose around which everything evolves.

Moon Our emotions, instincts, needs, and habitual responses, along with our home and early family life.

Mercury Communication, information, language, the mind.

Venus Love, relationships, pleasure, beauty, sustenance.

Mars Action, pursuit, lust, passion.

Jupiter Expansion, opportunity, education, freedom, travel.

Saturn Contraction, restriction, obstacles, boundaries, endings.

Uranus Innovation, unpredictability, eccentricity.

Neptune Imagination, illusion, glamour, escapism.

Pluto Transformation, rebirth, insight.

Chiron Healing, awakening.

The Planets and Their Dignities, Detriments, Exaltations, and Falls

Every planet has a sign or signs that it rules (see the chart on page 17). These are also known as the planet's sign(s) of *dignity*. The natures of the planet/sign are complementary and work together harmoniously. The opposite sign(s) are the planet's sign of *detriment*, in which the natures of the planet/sign are in conflict and struggle to understand each other. Note that this does not necessarily mean a simple split between "good" and "bad," but rather that there exists some friction or potential for conflict.

Every personal planet also has a sign in which it is said to be *exalted*, where it is arguably at its strongest placing. The sign opposite the sign of exaltation is the personal planet's sign of *fall*, its weakest placing, in which the natures of the planet/sign are mostly a mystery to each other.

Planet	Dignity	Detriment	Exaltation	Fall
Sun	Leo	Aquarius	Aries	Libra
Moon	Cancer	Capricorn	Taurus	Scorpio
Mercury	Gemini Virgo	Sagittarius Pisces	Virgo	Pisces
Venus	Taurus Libra	Scorpio Aries	Pisces	Virgo
Mars	Aries Scorpio	Libra Taurus	Capricorn	Cancer
Jupiter	Sagittarius Pisces	Gemini Virgo	Cancer	Capricorn
Saturn	Capricorn Aquarius	Cancer Leo	Libra	Aries
Uranus	Co-ruler of Aquarius	Leo	None	None
Neptune	Co-ruler of Pisces	Virgo	None	None
Pluto	Co-ruler of Scorpio	Taurus	None	None
Chiron	Possible co-ruler of Sagittarius	Gemini	None	None

Degree Positions

Here's a quick "back to school" mathematical reminder of the relationship between time and space.

- A clock face contains 360 degrees that are divided into 12 hours. Each hour contains 60 minutes (of time), and each minute contains 60 seconds (of time).
- The wheel of the horoscope contains 360 degrees and, as there are 12 signs of the zodiac, each sign contains 30 degrees. Each degree contains 60 minutes (of space), and each minute contains 60 seconds (of space).

So the degrees measure the precise location of a planet as it moves through a sign. Both 0 (beginnings) and 29 (endings) degrees are known as the "critical degrees" (see page 71).

Throughout this book, you will see shorthand versions of degree positions, for example "Moon 28 Sagittarius" refers to the Moon being positioned at 28 degrees of Sagittarius.

The Elements, the Modes, and the Aspects

Each sign has an associated element and mode. The assignment of an element and mode further singularizes the signs, illustrating and refining their essential temperament and the ways in which this is expressed.

The Elements

The four astrological elements are Fire, Earth, Air, and Water. Every fourth sign shares the same element, so there are three signs for each. These are known as the triplicities.

If you join up any three signs of the same triplicity, you will create an equilateral triangle. This is the first stepping stone toward understanding aspects (see page 21). Note that signs sharing the same element are in trine with one another—that is, they are compatible or harmonious (think "being in your element"). Here are the themes associated with each element:

- Fire: Warmth, passion, vision, intuition.
- Earth: Sensuality, practicality, fertility, materialism.
- Air: Thought, intellect, ideas, interaction.
- Water: Feelings, sensitivity, empathy, instinct.

Note that every Fire and Air sign is masculine and every Earth and Water sign is feminine.

The Modes

The three astrological modes are cardinal, fixed, and mutable. Every third sign shares the same mode, so there are four signs for each. These are known as the quadruplicities. If you join up any four signs of the same quadruplicity, you will create a square. Note that signs sharing the same mode are in "square" to one another (see page 21) and are incompatible or inharmonious.

- Cardinal: This mode represents the element in its most concentrated or active form. It is associated with push, energy, and initiation.
- Fixed: As the name suggests, this mode represents the element in its least changeable form. It is associated with stability or stubbornness.
- Mutable: Sometimes called "common," this mode represents the element at its most fluid. It is associated with flexibility, movement, and the dissemination of energy.

Elements and Modes in a Nutshell

♈ **Aries** Cardinal Fire, masculine

♉ **Taurus** Fixed Earth, feminine

♊ **Gemini** Mutable Air, masculine

♋ **Cancer** Cardinal Water, feminine

♌ **Leo** Fixed Fire, masculine

♍ **Virgo** Mutable Earth, feminine

♎ **Libra** Cardinal Air, masculine

♏ **Scorpio** Fixed Water, feminine

♐ **Sagittarius** Mutable Fire, masculine

♑ **Capricorn** Cardinal Earth, feminine

♒ **Aquarius** Fixed Air, masculine

♓ **Pisces** Mutable Water, feminine

The Aspects

Aspects tell us about the relationships between the signs and, therefore, the planets—whether or not they are connected, for good or ill, as allies or as enemies. Harmonious aspects generally reflect our happier personality traits and the areas of our lives that are easier and more pleasurable. The inharmonious aspects reflect the opposite—the troubled parts of our psyche and the areas of our lives that are characterized by tension or difficulty.

The Major Aspects

There are five major aspects—in terms of chart interpretation, all are important in delineating both character and destiny.

Conjunction Planets are positioned next to each other, sitting together (usually) in the same sign—harmonious or inharmonious, depending on the planets/signs involved.

Opposition Planets are 180 degrees (six signs) apart, i.e. in opposite signs—inharmonious, the opposition symbolizes conflict.

Trine Planets are 120 degrees (four signs) apart—a strong alliance, positive, helpful, and harmonious. Planets that are in trine are in the same element.

Square Planets are 90 degrees (three signs) apart—at odds with each other, stressful, a source of friction, inharmonious.

Sextile Planets are 60 degrees (two signs) apart—easy, friendly, and harmonious.

The Houses

The wheel of the horoscope is divided into 12 sections, called the Houses, which are a crucial part of astrological interpretation as they provide the context for the planets. In other words, when looking at an actual horoscope, we can immediately see where each planet "lives." The interpretation of any given planet in a sign is now further modified and enriched as we determine its particular role in the life of the individual or the "native," the person to whom the natal (birth) chart belongs.

The concerns of each House are in keeping with the symbolism of the sign and planet(s) to which they correspond and are numbered counterclockwise. So, as with the signs and planets, each House has its own dominion, whether this be other people, work matters, health issues, money, and so on.

In terms of astrological symmetry, the Houses work in pairs of opposites—for example, while the 1st House is about the individual, the opposite 7th House is about the significant other.

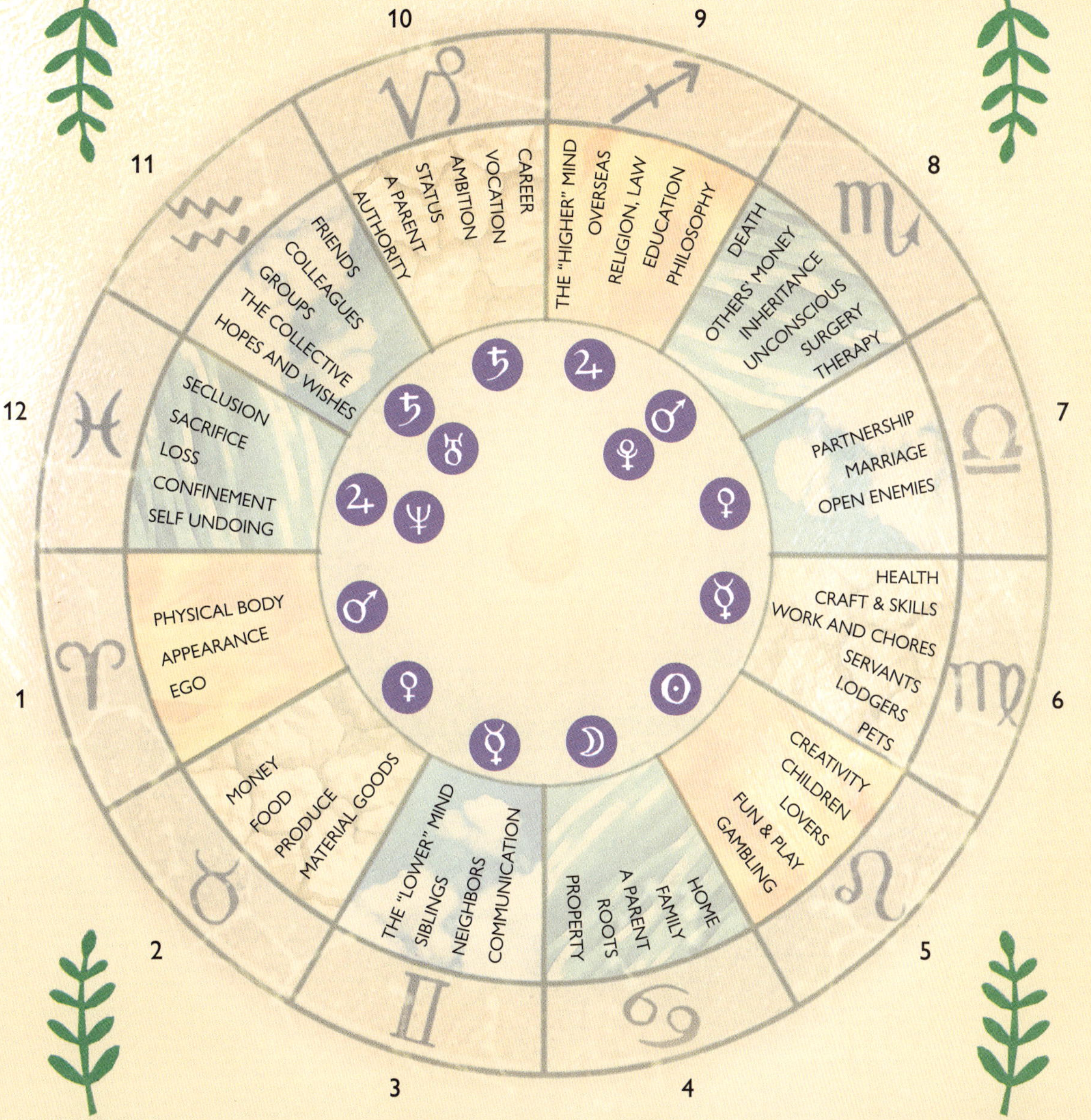
1
PHYSICAL BODY
APPEARANCE
EGO
2
MONEY
FOOD
PRODUCE
MATERIAL GOODS
3
THE "LOWER" MIND
SIBLINGS
NEIGHBORS
COMMUNICATION
4
HOME
FAMILY
A PARENT
ROOTS
PROPERTY
5
CREATIVITY
CHILDREN
LOVERS
FUN & PLAY
GAMBLING
6
HEALTH
CRAFT & SKILLS
WORK AND CHORES
SERVANTS
LODGERS
PETS
7
PARTNERSHIP
MARRIAGE
OPEN ENEMIES
8
DEATH
OTHERS' MONEY
INHERITANCE
UNCONSCIOUS
SURGERY
THERAPY
9
THE "HIGHER" MIND
OVERSEAS
RELIGION, LAW
EDUCATION
PHILOSOPHY
10
CAREER
VOCATION
AMBITION
STATUS
A PARENT
AUTHORITY
11
FRIENDS
COLLEAGUES
GROUPS
THE COLLECTIVE
HOPES AND WISHES
12
SECLUSION
SACRIFICE
LOSS
CONFINEMENT
SELF UNDOING

The Angles

If you draw a line from the beginning of the 1st House to the beginning of the 7th, and then from the beginning of the 4th to the beginning of the 10th, this axis marks out the all-important Angles of the chart. The subsequent trisection of the quadrants creates the inner House cusps and the 12 Houses. The Angles lock the chart into place—they're determined purely by the time of birth so they're highly sensitive to any astrological activity, including lunations (New and Full Moons). The wheel of the horoscope also acts as a 24-hour clock.

The Ascendant (06:00, Sunrise)

Arguably the most important part of the horoscope, the Ascendant—or rising sign—is the sign that was rising over the eastern horizon at the time of birth. It therefore marks the beginning of the 1st House and is the front door into any horoscope. The ruling planet of any horoscope is the planet that rules the sign on the Ascendant—for example, with an Aries Ascendant, the ruling planet of the horoscope is Mars. This planet acts as the native's particular "significator" and is of primary importance in both natal and predictive interpretation.

The Descendant (18:00, Sunset)

This Angle marks the beginning of the 7th House and is always exactly opposite the Ascendant. If the Ascendant is "me" then the Descendant is "you." This is where we locate any significant other in terms of partnership, personal or professional.

The Midheaven, or M.C. (Midday)

M.C. stands for Medium Coeli, which is the Latin phrase for "the middle of the sky." This Angle marks the beginning of the 10th House. In some horoscopes you will find this Angle drawn as an arrow, pointing up toward the heavens. So the Midheaven points to where we are going, symbolizing our vocation, status, and aspirations in life. In terms of people, this is where we find those who are above us, who rule over us, such as a boss or anyone in authority, and one of the parents.

The I.C. (Midnight)

I.C. stands for Imum Coeli, which is the Latin phrase for "the sky below us." This Angle is always exactly opposite the M.C., and it marks the beginning of the 4th House. It symbolizes our origins, where we have come from, along with all that pertains to home and property. In terms of people, this is where we find the other parent and generational issues.

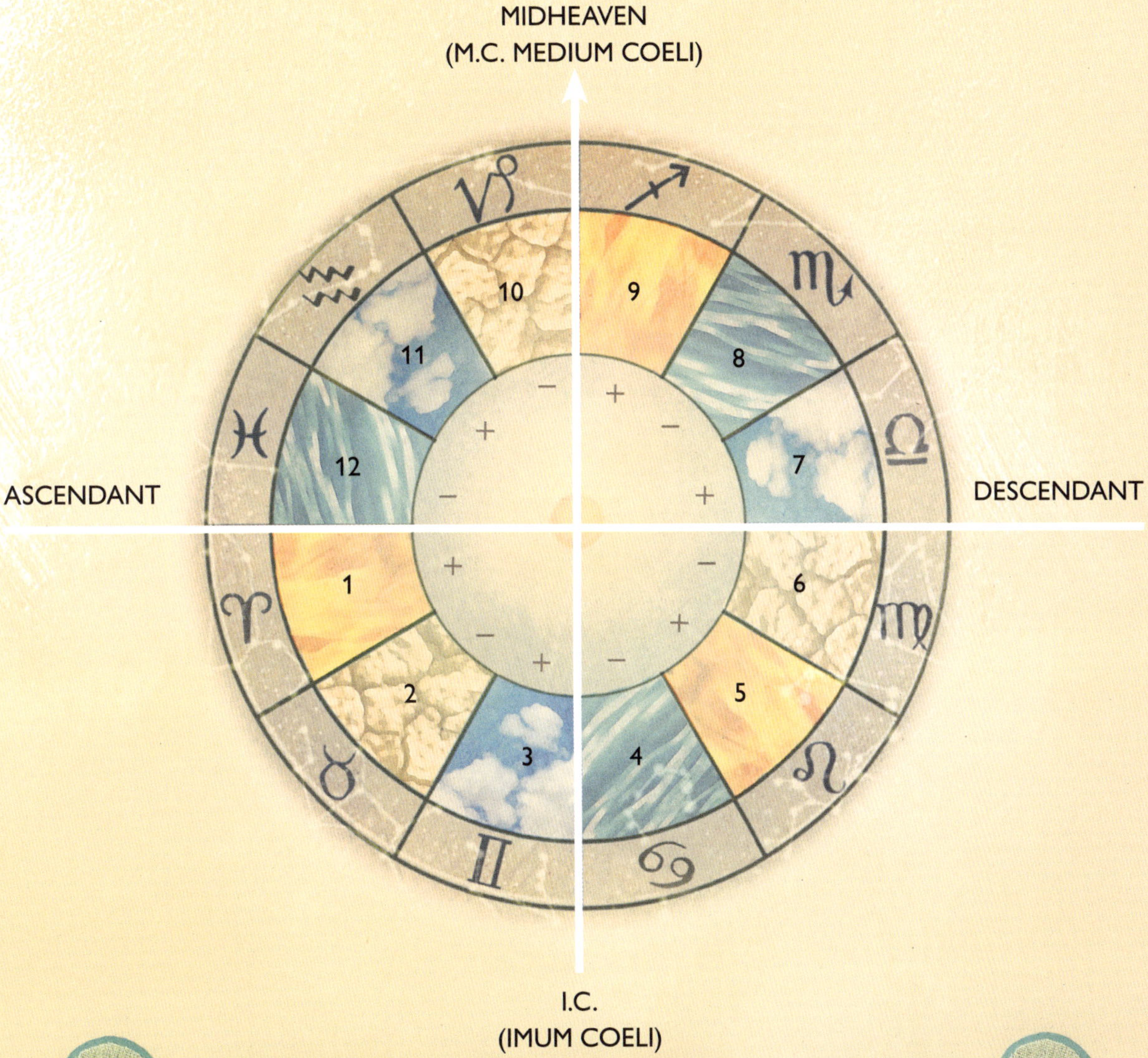

Chapter One

Moon Signs

Your Moon sign, or natal Moon, is determined by which zodiac sign the Moon was in at the time of your birth. Understanding the personality characteristics and common features of your own Moon sign, and of the people around you, will reveal a great deal about yourself and your relationships with others.

What Natal Moons Can Teach Us

Whenever someone asks me about astrological compatibility, they are nearly always referring to Sun signs. These are important, of course, but when it comes to daily life and emotional connections, the Moon is a far more vital consideration.

The Sun is our essential self, in many ways more visible and easier to understand, but it's the Moon who symbolizes our inner world and our deeper needs. She can also tell us a great deal more about our animal nature, such as the things that we do unconsciously or instinctively. The Moon can help us to make more sense of our childhood, the relationship with our mother or primary caregiver, how and where we feel safe or unsafe, how we like our home to be, and how we function best in daily life. The Moon is also the swiftest moving body, taking just 29 days to do the same journey that takes the Sun a whole year, so where she lands in any given horoscope has the ring of fine timing.

Have you ever noticed how everyone loves their Sun sign? Even those who know very little or no astrology will announce their own sign in a proprietorial way. When we identify with and connect with our Moon sign, too, that ownership becomes even stronger, showing us how to self-parent and meet those needs that maybe weren't always, or ever, met in our childhood. Seeing how this is true of others, too, is a wonderful path toward the giving and receiving of unconditional love, remembering that every single one of us was once a child.

Synastry

In addition to learning about the Moon signs individually, there's another layer of astrology called synastry. This is astro-speak for compatibility, for good or ill, as revealed through the comparison of two horoscopes. This is a process of matching up the two sets of planets to locate areas of harmony or discord, including spiritual or karmic connections. It can explain a lot!

The Cosmic Marriage

One of the key techniques is to note when one person's Sun is in the same sign as another person's Moon. This is called the "cosmic marriage," personal or professional. According to traditional astrology, the union of the Lights (the Sun and the Moon) speaks of a destined connection and the rules of astrological craft say that the two bodies should be no more than 5 degrees (see page 18) apart. Here are some clear examples of this rule (correct at the time of writing).

- King Charles III (Moon 0 Taurus) and the late Queen Elizabeth II (Sun 0 Taurus) are firstborn child and mother.
- Jeff Bezos (Moon 28 Sagittarius) and Lauren Sanchez (Sun 28 Sagittarius) have been married since 2025.
- Britney Spears (Moon 12 Aquarius) and Justin Timberlake (Sun 12 Aquarius) dated for three years.
- David Bowie (Moon 3 Leo) and Iman (Sun 2 Leo) were married for 23 years until Bowie's death.
- Elizabeth Taylor (Moon 15 Scorpio) and Richard Burton (Sun 17 Scorpio) were married twice, totalling around 11 years.
- Jennifer Aniston (Moon 23 Sagittarius) and Brad Pitt (Sun 25 Sagittarius) were married for five years.
- Carter Reum (Moon 27 Aquarius) and Paris Hilton (Sun 28 Aquarius) have been married since 2021.
- Orlando Bloom (Moon 0 Scorpio) and Katy Perry (Sun 2 Scorpio) were in a relationship for nine years.
- Adele (Moon 26 Sagittarius) and Rich Paul (Sun 24 Sagittarius) have been in a relationship since 2021, getting engaged in 2024.
- Travis Kelce (Moon 15 Sagittarius) (Noon chart, see page 140) and Taylor Swift (Sun 15 Sagittarius) have been in a relationship since 2023, getting engaged in 2025.

However, over the years, I've found that the cosmic marriage clearly works when we see the Lights as a pairing, regardless of how many degrees apart they may be. Here are some examples of when the Lights are more than 5 degrees apart.

- Prince Harry, Duke of Sussex (Moon 21 Taurus) and Prince Archie of Sussex (Sun 15 Taurus) are father and firstborn child.
- Paul Newman (Moon 1 Pisces) and Joanne Woodward (Sun 8 Pisces) were married for 50 years until Newman's death.
- John Lennon (Moon 3 Aquarius) and Yoko Ono (Sun 29 Aquarius) were married for 11 years until Lennon's death.
- Julian Lennon (Moon 9 Libra) and John Lennon (Sun 16 Libra) are firstborn child and father.
- Dustin Hoffman (Moon 18 Virgo) and Lisa Hoffman (Sun 8 Virgo) have been married for 44 years but have known each other longer, since Lisa was a child.
- Pierre Curie (Moon 2 Scorpio) and Marie Curie (Sun 14 Scorpio) were married for nearly 11 years until Pierre's death, and had a legendary scientific work partnership.
- Audrey Hepburn (Moon 6 Pisces) and Hubert de Givenchy (Sun 0 Pisces) had a friendship spanning four decades, (he described her as a sister, she described him as her best friend).
- Caroline, Princess of Hanover (Moon 8 Scorpio) and Grace Kelly (Sun 19 Scorpio) are firstborn child and mother.

Famous On-Screen Couples

The cosmic marriage describes a chemistry between two people of the kind that movie directors pray for. Casting is everything in the world of film, especially when it comes to comic timing or in iconic love stories that need to be utterly compelling and believable. The following movie stars appeared together in well-known on-screen romantic relationships.

- Marilyn Monroe (Moon 19 Aquarius) and Jack Lemmon (Sun 19 Aquarius) costarred as Sugar Kane and Jerry/Daphne in *Some Like It Hot*.
- Vivien Leigh (Moon 9 Aquarius) and Clark Gable (Sun 12 Aquarius) costarred as Scarlett O'Hara and Rhett Butler in *Gone with the Wind*.
- Dustin Hoffman (Moon 18 Virgo) and Anne Bancroft (Sun 23 Virgo) costarred as Benjamin Braddock and Mrs Robinson in *The Graduate*.
- Leonardo DiCaprio (Moon 15 Libra) and Kate Winslet (Sun 11 Libra) costarred as Jack and Rose in *Titanic*.

Sharing the Same Moon Sign

Look out, too, for pairings of individuals who have the Moon in the same sign, as this is also an indication of special compatibility and relationship longevity in romance, friendship, or professionally.

- Queen Elizabeth II and Prince Philip, Duke of Edinburgh (Moon in Leo). They were married for over 73 years—the longest royal marriage in history—until his death.
- William and Catherine, Prince and Princess of Wales (Moon in Cancer).
- Tina Turner and Erwin Bach (Moon in Gemini).
- Tom Hanks and Rita Wilson (Moon in Leo).
- Marilyn Monroe and Arthur Miller (Moon in Aquarius).
- Matthew Perry and Lisa Kudrow (Moon in Scorpio).
- Diane Keaton and Woody Allen (Moon in Aquarius).
- Ava Gardner and Frank Sinatra (Moon in Pisces).

As you read about the individual natal signs, you'll recognize characteristics and habits—your own and those of the people closest to you. These can go a long way toward explaining why people are the way they are, unraveling a great deal about early experiences and how these have shaped the nature that we see today. You can also explore the emotional makeup and patterns in your own family, to understand the dynamics at work or even see if there are any themes being handed down through the generations.

If you have any Moon synastry with those who are important to you, this will add another rich layer to understanding the celestial DNA at work, and remind you that there are no accidents or coincidences in the business of incarnation. Moon astrology is packed with information about why our relationships are all different, about everything we're here to learn from others, and what they are here to learn from us.

Astrological Relationship between Mother and Firstborn

It is notable how often a firstborn child has their mother's Sun sign as their Moon sign. Let's use the British royal family as a striking example of this theme working out through four consecutive generations.

- Queen Elizabeth the Queen Mother was Sun in Leo; firstborn child daughter Queen Elizabeth II was Moon in Leo.
- Queen Elizabeth II was Sun in Taurus; firstborn child son King Charles III is Moon in Taurus.
- Diana, Princess of Wales was Sun in Cancer; firstborn child son William, Prince of Wales is Moon in Cancer.
- Catherine, Princess of Wales is Sun in Capricorn; firstborn child son Prince George is Moon in Capricorn.

Moon in Aries

Element: Fire

Mode: Cardinal

Ruler: Mars

Symbol: The Ram

Key phrase: I am

Personality Traits

The Moon in the first sign of the zodiac is a sizzler—fervent, impatient, and usually several steps ahead of everyone else. You would expect no less from leader of the pack Aries, a Fire sign ruled by red hot Mars, the god of war, who symbolizes everything to do with action and how we arm ourselves for battle.

Individuals with this Moon can pick a fight faster than anyone, sometimes deliberately, but mostly because of the need to do things immediately, quickly, and efficiently. They have a combative streak that leaps to the fore when frustrated, angered, or simply when they want something, and they're a one-person army when it comes to a cherished cause or defending a loved one. In that respect, it follows that they make fantastic friends in a crisis, and they'll fight your corner with fierce loyalty. They're the first to volunteer and they're probably one of the first people you'd call on when you need help. Aries does "firsts" in every sense.

In the physical body, Aries rules the head and face. So, the flip side to the coin can be a tendency to be in your face, to go in headfirst, without taking any time to consider the consequences. When it comes to steamrollering, they're in a league of their own. Headstrong or defiant behavior can land them in hot water, but they feel only the immediate need rather than thinking of the longer term, or even the short term, repercussions. When they're in full-blown militant mode it's very hard, if not impossible, to say no to this Moon.

That warrior energy is unmatchable when it comes to personal achievement. These individuals often feel driven to make their mark on the world—they have the need to lead and the desire to excel. Individuals with this Moon are often natural pioneers. Both Bill Gates of Microsoft and the late Steve Jobs of Apple have this Moon and their work has changed the face of technology, and the lives of millions, forever.

In Relationships

As the leader of the zodiacal pack, Aries rules the ego and the self, a correlation that can lead us straight into the trap of putting two and two together and making five. An Aries Moon doesn't necessarily or automatically translate into selfishness in the sense of not caring about anyone else—often, it's quite the contrary.

There can be a marked singlemindedness that manifests as extreme loyalty and total commitment to "the one." A Capricorn client with an Aries Moon only ever had one boyfriend—she was brokenhearted when he left her and married someone else. She waited several years, staying celibate, convinced he was her soulmate and that he would return. He did. They have a successful marriage and children.

Singer Celine Dion is a double Aries, Sun and Moon in this sign, along with Saturn, who often indicates an older partner. Her love story with her manager and then husband, music producer René Angélil, 26 years her senior, is famous. She auditioned

for him when she was just 12 years old and never looked at another man from that moment on. Until they became a couple, in secret when she was 19, she slept with a photo of René under her pillow. Since his death in 2016, Celine has so far, at the time of writing, stayed single (at least publicly).

However, given that this Moon is programmed for self-protection, there are lessons to be learned along the way about the art of genuine negotiation; how the best outcome isn't always about getting our own way. These individuals are a joy to be around when everyone is agreeing with them or admiring them, but hallmarks of a troubled Aries Moon is a "me first" attitude, a neediness for a lot of external validation, or even tantrums. It's hardly surprising that this Moon is attracted to passive partners, or that others often give in to them just to keep the peace, leading to a "spoiled child" syndrome, where their needs are met at the expense of everyone else's.

If you're in conflict with this Moon, let them speak first—not that you'll have any choice, but don't leave it there. They'll think that the conversation is over, but it isn't. Have your say. You can cement a deep and lifelong connection with this person when you win their respect.

Other Moon in Aries Celebrities

- Aries Sun: Marlon Brando
- Aries Sun: Brigitte Macron
- Gemini Sun: Angelina Jolie
- Gemini Sun: Novak Djokovic
- Leo Sun: Daniel Radcliffe
- Leo Sun: Jacqueline Kennedy Onassis
- Leo Sun: Whitney Houston
- Libra Sun: Kamala Harris
- Sagittarius Sun: Tyra Banks
- Aquarius Sun: Ellen DeGeneres

Moon in Taurus

Element: Earth

Mode: Fixed

Ruler: Venus

Symbol: The Bull

Key phrase: I possess

Personality Traits

The Moon rules the Water sign of Cancer, but she's exalted in the fertile, earthy Taurus, Venus's feminine sign, planet of love, money, and pleasures. So, the Moon Taurus combination is sensual, generally contented as long as they're not broke and usually low on drama as long as you don't hassle them. Or drop things on them at short notice. Unpredictability unsettles this Moon, so if you want them to do something for you, or with you, give them plenty of advance warning. Several days or even longer works well. However, this Moon is one of the best for being there when genuinely needed and will sit through a crisis to the bitter end.

Individuals with this Moon attach great value to their creature comforts, often to the extent of finding it difficult to tolerate any kind of discomfort—physical or emotional. Sometimes this side to their nature links to a lazy streak, or simply an intense dislike of rocking the boat. They need peace, familiarity, and are comfortable with routine.

It's one of those astrological myths that all Earth signs are practical and sensible. Sometimes they have bags of common sense, sometimes they don't—this varies depending on other astrological factors. This exalted Moon, however, nearly always indicates an ability to create financial security or a beautiful home, or both, if these things haven't already been handed down to them.

There's often an acquisitive streak to this Moon, whether it's collecting objects of beauty or a dislike of throwing anything away. A Taurus Moon client told me that her home is beautiful but full of junk and it's her partner who's the hoarder who, guess what, also has a Taurus Moon. Too much attachment to the material world, compulsive shopping or eating, or other addictions can be this Moon's downfall.

A healthy Taurus Moon often shows in a pronounced link to nature. This is the Moon sign of King Charles III (Sun in Scorpio), who has always been known for his love of agriculture and for being a pioneer of organic farming, not to mention talking to plants. In 1986, that comment was met with ridicule, but is now regarded as visionary.

In Relationships

This beautiful Moon is, unsurprisingly, a big plus for steady and lasting relationships. These individuals have a placidity about them; they know how to create a stable homelife. They're often the breadwinner in a relationship, or they're drawn to partners who will be reliable providers. Either way, the security of knowing that the cupboards will never be empty and that the bills can always be met is a must. Wasters and daydreamers need not apply. Financial problems can make them physically ill.

This Moon has extremely strong survival instincts, a healthy sexual appetite, and staying power—all strong ingredients in the recipe for successful long-term relationships. The flip side is that valuing familiarity over the unknown can translate into scoring low on the excitement scale, which can sometimes become an issue. Over the years, I've encountered Taurus Moon people who've stayed with a partner for what they very privately think to be the wrong reasons. Either the relationship had become boring, or life with their partner had always been safe but dull from the outset, but they wouldn't dream of telling them so.

It's a price that a Taurus Moon is often willing to pay. The risk of jeopardizing their quality of life, fear of change, the guilt of upsetting the family dynamics—these are the kind of things that tick the "stay put" Taurus boxes even when the physical intimacy has stopped. Or, the other, but not so frequent, pattern with this Moon is to separate amicably after many years when mutual priorities change.

Throughout her Hollywood career, Sun in Cancer actress Meryl Streep has been known for a rock-solid homelife. Cancer rules home, family, and protection. She separated very privately from husband Don Gummer in 2017—but that was after 40 years of marriage and four children—and is quoted as saying she was "wired for family." The influential bond with her own mother comes across loud and clear, with Meryl citing her as her first mentor, the woman who fed her with powerful self-belief and confidence from a very young age.

These individuals are not known for being emotional risk-takers. It can take a long time to get to know them, but once the commitment is in place and the barriers go down, the rewards are immense. This Moon describes someone who is loyal, a skilled lover, and funny. They effectively use humor to get through the difficult times.

Other Moon in Taurus Celebrities

- Aries Sun: Elton John
- Aries Sun: Gregory Peck
- Taurus Sun: Kelly Clarkson
- Cancer Sun: Nicole Scherzinger
- Leo Sun: Monica Lewinsky
- Leo Sun: Bill Clinton
- Virgo Sun: Prince Harry, Duke of Sussex
- Virgo Sun: Cameron Diaz
- Virgo Sun: Colin Firth
- Virgo Sun: Hugh Grant

Moon in Gemini

Element: Air

Mode: Mutable

Ruler: Mercury

Symbol: The Twins

Key phrase: I speak

Personality Traits

The zodiac signs as a chain of continual opposites now starts to become apparent. Aries is direct and immediate, Taurus is slow and deliberate, while Gemini is simply all over the place—endearingly funny and nutty on a good day, disorganized or scatterbrained on a bad one. Paradoxically, this Moon can actually be very focused on the task at hand, as long as it's interesting.

These individuals have "butterfly minds," flitting from one subject to the next with ease, but they're perfectly capable of giving you their full attention when they engage with you, but only because it's your turn. Just don't take all day about it and get to the point. Belonging to Mercury, winged messenger of the gods, the top need of this airy and restless Moon is to be in constant circulation and communication, so the exclusive connection doesn't last long. They've got a hundred other things to do.

If you want to understand this Moon's psyche and secret world, think Peter Pan—quick, clever, and elusive, the eternal youth with no intention of growing up. Gemini Moon people tend to age well. They have a childlike mobility in their facial expressions, a curiosity about everything, and know a little about a lot but, again, the assumption that they're jack-of-all-trades and master of none is usually wide of the mark.

A consistently present hallmark of the sign of the Twins is any kind of duality or multiplicity, and these Moon people are multitasking but often multitalented, too. They can turn their hand to anything or possess a marked dexterity with those fiddly little jobs that require nimble fingers.

Gemini's job of language learning and communicating is arguably the biggest clue of all to the workings of this live-wire Moon. This is former US President Barack Obama's

Moon. Apart from that center stage role (Sun in Leo) that ensured his place in history, he's also famous for the gift of mesmerizing oratory. He has an engaging voice and his speech after his first presidential victory in 2008 is considered as one of the best of the 21st century.

In Relationships

The one thing that this lively and mischievous Moon sign does not need in life is just a partner, especially one who is possessive or easily jealous. If you fall for someone with this Moon, and then expect to be the center of their world to the exclusion of all else, you'll definitely be hitching your star to the wrong wagon.

This Moon signifies someone with a larger than average number of friends or outside interests, or both. These are their sources of stimulus and variety that feed a hunger for company and for learning. They may also be the kind who loves to sit down with a pile of books but, either way, new information is food for this Moon's mind and soul.

Gemini is wired for twinship and loves to join forces, but it has to be with a like-minded other, someone who also has their own interests and who can make them laugh. On that subject, they do have to guard against using humor as a way of deflecting real intimacy, and may have to acquire more serious communication skills.

However, once you get past those barriers, this "up for anything" Moon is heaven sent for exploring the weird, wonderful, or emotional.

In the words of one of my Moon Gemini clients, "I get frustrated when I don't understand something so it really helps me to talk things through; I'm good at articulating (Gemini) my feelings and needs (Moon)."

Wherever we find Gemini, duality is never far behind. With the Moon's connection to early environment, this can show as things like two homes, or two sets of parents, or being raised bilingual. In adult life, we see either the serial dater, or at least two marriages or significant relationships, with the second or later one usually being the most successful and even part of a total reinvention.

This was singer Tina Turner's Moon, opposite her Sun in Sagittarius, which means that she was born on a Full Moon (see page 114). Her years of domestic violence with first husband Ike are well-documented. She ran for her life. She wrote of her second husband Erwin Bach that he restored her faith in humanity, donating one of his kidneys to rescue her from the life sentence of dialysis. A Gemini Moon can signal a big difference in ages and Aquarian Erwin was born January 24, 1956, making him 16 years her junior. He also has Moon in Gemini, and they were together for 37 years.

Other Moon in Gemini Celebrities

- Pisces Sun: Simone Biles
- Pisces Sun: Anita Moorjani
- Capricorn Sun: Jim Carrey
- Scorpio Sun: Goldie Hawn
- Capricorn Sun: Rowan Atkinson
- Libra Sun: Groucho Marx
- Libra Sun: Gwyneth Paltrow
- Libra Sun: Hugh Jackman
- Gemini Sun: Kylie Minogue
- Gemini Sun: Heidi Klum

Moon in Cancer

Element: Water

Mode: Cardinal

Ruler: The Moon

Symbol: The Crab

Key phrase: I secure

Personality Traits

Cancer is the only sign actually ruled by the Moon so, as we would expect, the connections between the two are especially strong. However, while this Moon sign has many strengths, it also has many vulnerabilities, and is not as easy to understand as we might at first think.

The Moon in any sign speaks of the childhood experience, family lineage, and especially the maternal relationship, but the Cancer Moon arrives with these themes highlighted and in bold. The mother's role and influence will definitely be notable, for good or ill, depending on how this Moon sits in relation to the other planets (people) in a person's horoscope (life). In other words, the Moon in her sign of dignity doesn't automatically indicate all the blessings and none of the blights.

So, a happy Cancer Moon in harmony with other planets indicates a very strong early environment—an emotionally secure start in life, with one or both parents able to nurture their child and meet their particular needs. Deep bonds of attachment are forged. With this kind of role model, these Moon individuals naturally bring their own caring and healing skills into the world.

An unhappy Cancer Moon indicates an unhealthy parental relationship. This can be anywhere on the scale from an overly sheltered upbringing to neglect, indifference, the wounding of broken homes, or the loss of a parent through abandonment or bereavement. The result is a story of having to learn how to self-parent and figure out life for themselves.

Either way, parenting, protection, and family life are definitive themes for this highly sensitive Moon. If they lack immediate family then they'll create one—their own clan that is carefully selected.

In terms of the famous crab shell, there's a tendency to self-isolate when feeling hurt or overwhelmed by the world. Nobody can turn home into a fortress like the sign of the Crab but, once they let you in, there's no greater welcome either. Just don't move away. Or forget to show appreciation. This can be a touchy or tearful Moon if there's a whisper of being discarded, or taken for granted.

In Relationships

No sign has exclusive rights to sensitivity, but astrologically we know that we're on delicate emotional ground when we find the Moon in Cancer, or indeed in any of the Water signs. Those with a Cancer Moon are usually acutely aware of their own highly emotional nature, but equally aware of the fact that this isn't always obvious to others. They can easily feel misunderstood, alone, or even victimized.

To be fair to those "others," from family through to newcomers, this Moon sign is not the easiest when it comes to getting close. The hard shell of the exterior image is a tough one, a highly effective suit of armor that works at many levels, protecting that soft center and providing a crawl space of retreat when life or the demands of relationships become too painful. It's virtually a knee-jerk reaction to be secretive, especially when showing their true feelings.

Moon in Cancer is tenacious and rarely gives up or lets go. The downside to that is clingy behavior if they feel a loved one pulling away, or a tendency to brood over grievances or old hurts, but they also procrastinate. Only the most extreme kind of betrayal would make them unhook.

Put all that together with the Crab's "sideways" nature that tends to body swerve any kind of directness, and we find that quality relationships for this Moon are inevitably the ones that develop slowly, gently, and cautiously. They need a lot of empathy. Keep clearing the air. The reward is entering their sanctum of loving security that is hard to equal, emotionally and materially. This Moon is wired for a long-term partnership, and once they've found their soulmate, there's no turning back. This Moon is a natural homemaker and very often there's a tale of acquiring some kind of special property, especially one to share with a partner and to leave for future generations.

Scorpio Kris Jenner exemplifies the Moon in Cancer's role as the matriarch and the strong bonds to family concerns. With her Moon in the 10th House (career), she rose to fame and fortune with *Keeping up with the Kardashians*, a long running reality TV series that followed the lives of herself and her six children.

Other Moon in Cancer Celebrities

- Cancer Sun: William, Prince of Wales
- Cancer Sun: Queen Camilla
- Cancer Sun: Harrison Ford
- Leo Sun: Princess Margaret
- Virgo Sun: Keanu Reeves
- Scorpio Sun: Keith Urban
- Sagittarius Sun: Taylor Swift
- Capricorn Sun: Catherine, Princess of Wales
- Capricorn Sun: Carolyn Bessette Kennedy
- Pisces Sun: Drew Barrymore
- Pisces Sun: Liza Minnelli

Moon in Leo

Element: Fire

Mode: Fixed

Ruler: The Sun

Symbol: The Lion

Key phrase: I create

Personality Traits

The Moon in the Sun's sign reminds us that these two bodies are inextricably linked. They're the source of our light by night or day, and they symbolize the essence of life itself. So, there's a particular vibrancy about those born under a Leo Moon, whether it's full-on or subtle. On a good day, they're the hosts with the most—they can warm up a room just by walking into it and you'd pay them to come to your party. They can connect instantly with anyone, adult or child. Or animals. It's notable that every single name on this Moon's celebrities list is known either for being passionate about animals or for being a dedicated animal welfare activist.

A bad day is just as obvious. The light dims, they can be aloof in that "don't bother me" kind of way, and they'll be on a short fuse—making a drama out of something trivial, or just very quiet and sad. This can be due to burnout and the need to recharge, or it's frustration with themselves, other people, or a matter they can't resolve, or which frightens them, but they're usually too proud to say so.

This Moon describes a nature that is extremely competent; these individuals don't admit defeat easily. They thrive on achievement, invariably linked to their awesome creative or organizational skills, and on other people's positive regard. They're generous and supportive, but allergic to being told what to do, or to ridicule. They're not that great at handling disappointment either. It brings out the petulant child in them.

Leo the Lion is the royal sign, ruling the kings and queens of the zodiac as well as the jungle. There's a tad of the thespian (drama) or diva ("don't you know who I am?") behavior in every Leo Moon, or Sun, and they have to learn to tone it down and value other people's time. In appearance, we often see that "look" of strong leonine physical characteristics, such as a regal bearing or the mane—rich, shaggy, distinctive locks can pick out the looks of either sex. Singer George Michael (Cancer Sun) and actress Julia Roberts (Scorpio Sun) are two prime examples.

In Relationships

The Moon's link to the Sun is known as a dyadic relationship, two parts being forever connected, interdependent, and making a whole. This is easily illustrated by the fact that it's only because of the solar–lunar relationship that we have New/Full Moons and Eclipses.

Understand this symbolically crucial cog in the Leo Moon's wheel, and so many other things drop into place. Two is the smallest possible social group and these individuals need their "significant other," without whom they cannot shine. Many have an early experience of an exclusive relationship of mutual adoration, the person without whom life would be unthinkable. Often, it's one of the parents, but not always. For one of my clients, it was her twin sister—they were each other's world from the womb onward. For another, it was her grandmother, who was an unflagging source of love and positive regard until the day she died.

Whether they're conscious of it or not, Moon in Leo individuals seek to replicate that total acceptance and contentment in other relationships, an extremely difficult or impossible task. In this respect, this is a naive Moon. Placing their unquestioning, childlike trust in the wrong people brings painful lessons that they may have to learn several times over. The Leo confidence in life and love is not a given as we're led to believe, but hard-won through experience.

When wounded or adrift with no emotional compass, a Leo Moon retreats into the lion's den. Don't be surprised if there's silence while they recover. They gradually come back to life again once they've licked their wounds, but this Moon can be very private about personal pain. At such times, these house (Moon) proud (Leo) individuals often finds therapy in cleaning, and they'll emerge from a gleaming den, not squalor.

There's nothing sadder than an unloved Leo Moon but, when a true connection is made, there's nothing more glorious. If you want to get close to a Leo Moon person then just bring on your A game—attention, affection, admiration, adoration—and you'll get past their cover story of not needing anyone, thank you.

Leo rules the heart, the emotional one as well as the physical. A Leo Moon is naturally wholehearted, but if they're not Top Cat, the relationship will wither and die. So, no game-playing. It's all or nothing. Open your heart and absolutely nothing will take away Leo loyalty, no matter what life may throw at you. This Moon is in for the long haul.

Other Moon in Leo Celebrities

- Aquarius Sun: Charlene, Princess of Monaco
- Taurus Sun: Barbra Streisand
- Taurus Sun: Queen Elizabeth II
- Gemini Sun: Prince Philip, Duke of Edinburgh
- Gemini Sun: Clint Eastwood
- Gemini Sun: Helena Bonham Carter
- Gemini Sun: Paul McCartney
- Cancer Sun: Tom Hanks
- Libra Sun: Mahatma Gandhi
- Scorpio Sun: Rita Wilson
- Sagittarius Sun: Jane Fonda
- Capricorn Sun: David Bowie

Moon in Virgo

Element: Earth

Mode: Mutable

Ruler: Mercury

Symbol: The Maiden

Key phrase: I serve

Personality Traits

A Virgo Moon excels at presenting the perfectly packaged image, but don't be fooled. Under the smooth surface of stillness there's always a churning machinery of activity. These individuals are far more complex than they at first appear and that outward reserve is a mask for a nature that battles with conflict and anxiety. This makes sense when we consider that the stuff of life is a messy business, a fact that is hugely at odds with the Virgo love of neatness, precision, certainty, and good health.

Often it's the need to impose order on a chaotic world, or especially on their own inner turmoil, that can manifest in fussiness, at both an aesthetic and hygienic level. This can be anything from naturally keeping everything clean and tidy right through to OCD (obsessive-compulsive disorder), when the slightest thing out of place disturbs their equilibrium.

Early homelife is nearly always a difficult time, either because of parents always working or experiences that make the child feel vulnerable, existing only to serve others, or "not good enough." The Virgo Moon for one of my clients sprang to life when she described her anxiety-ridden mother as constantly critical, negative, and needy, capturing the fretful and troubled side to this sign. "Childhood" had been about keeping mother calm.

In terms of strengths, Virgo is also the sign of crafts and skills, and is known for hard work and perfectionism. Unsurprisingly, we find this Moon among top businesspeople, specialists, and hugely talented artistes. The celebrities list includes actors who are recognized as the greatest of their generation, or even of all time.

On that theme, underachieving is a disaster for this Moon. They're their own biggest critics. Creating financial security is vital for their sense of security but by far the strongest motivation is the need to excel at whatever they do. That sweet taste of success, of getting it right, is crucial for their satisfaction with life, and themselves. Leo Sun, Virgo Moon, self-made billionaire author J. K. Rowling has produced a unique wealth of detailed, creative work, yet has also shared that failure is her biggest fear.

In Relationships

On first meeting, what you see is definitely not what you get. The Virgo Moon cover story is one of self-containment, to the extent that they can come across as shy, even inhibited or oh-so cool. More usually, they're none of the above, but they'll let down their guard only when they feel completely safe and accepted.

The Virgo Moon list of needs is extensive. It's also a juggling act of contradictions. On the one hand, they need gentleness, quietness, and unwavering approval. When stressed or anxious—virtually their default setting—they need smoothing and soothing. On the other hand, they need plenty of meaningful conversation and mental stimulation. After all, this is a communicative Mercury sign, and Virgo's mental cogs never stop turning. Their powers of analysis are second to none, from a tendency to over scrutinize just about everything through to deeply insightful observations. On a good day, they can get the measure of a new person or situation in seconds and come up with brilliant ideas, but on a bad day, they overwhelm themselves with the details.

The ideal partner for this Moon sign is someone low on drama and high on humor. When prompted to keep things in perspective and not to take everything so seriously, life becomes a whole lot more manageable. Their own clever wit comes to life when reminded that life is something that they're supposed to be enjoying.

If you have someone with this Moon in your household, there's a lot to navigate. Usually, they set very high standards and don't cope easily with having their own routines and rituals disrupted. One Virgo Moon client told me that every bottle in her bathroom was arranged in descending order of size. Whoever coined the phrase of "a place for everything and everything in its place" must have had this Moon!

However, the most important thing about homelife is that it must be a sanctuary. These individuals need time to process their thoughts and emotions, especially if they're irritable or stinging from criticism. When home is clean, comfortable, decluttered, and a place for making good memories, that is a Virgo Moon paradise. Throw in exclusivity, too. This Moon does fidelity, and is unforgiving if it's not mutual.

Other Moon in Virgo Celebrities

- Taurus Sun: Jack Nicholson
- Taurus Sun: Laurence Olivier
- Taurus Sun: Shirley MacLaine
- Gemini Sun: Courteney Cox
- Cancer Sun: Elon Musk
- Cancer Sun: Richard Branson
- Leo Sun: Dustin Hoffman
- Leo Sun: Robert Redford
- Scorpio Sun: Jodie Foster
- Capricorn Sun: Stephen Hawking

Moon in Libra

Element: Air

Mode: Cardinal

Ruler: Venus

Symbol: The Scales

Key phrase: I relate

Personality Traits

We arrive at the halfway point of the zodiac, so considering the opposite sign provides a wealth of insights. As the leader of the pack, Aries is the sign of the self, the initiator, and the warrior. Thus Libra is the sign of "the other," the considerer of options, and the peacemaker.

Individuals with this Moon therefore tend to lack any obvious sense of urgency or immediacy, and in that respect they're very easy and comfortable to be with. The flip side is that they can be the ultimate procrastinators. You'll know you're in lazy Libran airspace when you constantly hear the words, "I'll think about it," "I'll do it later," or "I'm not sure, what do *you* think?" Somehow, they *do* get things done, but in their own good time and when the conditions feel right.

The sign of the Scales weighs things up, with all the attendant indecision, hesitation, or dithering that go with the process. Too many choices can be overwhelming, a point that is especially worth noting for children with this Moon. In adult life, whether a dilemma is something major or minor, overthinking is often linked either to the worry of making the wrong decision or sticking to the one they thought they'd finally made. They can drive you nuts, but that's nothing compared to what they do to themselves.

The Scales symbolize justice, too. This Moon has a definite concern with fairness, both for themselves and in the way that others are treated. Their long fuse burns out fast when rising up in defense of their loved ones or a humanitarian cause.

Otherwise, though, the laid-back Venusian factor is usually very much in evidence, in the blessings of a lovely nature, an ability to talk to anyone, and a talent for teamwork. Beauty is important, too, whether it's their own look, home decor, or their neighborhood, to the extent that ugliness of any kind can depress them. Venus' work of beautifying is evident in the horoscopes of famous designers, such as Louis Vuitton, Pierre Cardin, Hubert de Givenchy, and Miuccia Prada, who all have this Moon.

In Relationships

The symbolism of the Scales now takes on greater significance, with the two sides being inextricably linked in perpetual partnership. Libra is *the* sign of relating, to the extent that it's unusual for individuals with this Moon to be single for long periods of time. They enjoy the coupled world of sharing, togetherness, and companionship —sexual or platonic.

With the right partner, they enter easily into the pleasures and the work of wholehearted commitment. As with all things in life, they're attracted to beauty and elegance, but that doesn't mean superficiality. Many find their soulmate. Sun Pisces, Moon Libra actor Michael Caine married his wife Shakira in January 1973 and consistently refers to her as "the other half of me."

What about the wrong partner? A Libra Moon is, unfortunately, never a fail-safe recipe for romantic success. This Venus sign can be easily seduced by the lure of romance, strong sexual attraction, a longing for children, or the fear of being alone. Early relationships or first marriages that go wrong are huge Libra lessons. Love turning

sour is a bitter pill for this romantic Moon, provoking deep soul-searching about their own judgment and counting the financial costs in dismay.

However, once these periods of disillusionment pass, a Libra Moon doesn't need much encouragement to reenter the love arena. Sun Aquarius, Moon Libra former astronaut Buzz Aldrin got married for the fourth time at the age of 93. Those who stay single in later life usually do so by conscious choice.

Libra Moon individuals are naturally sociable, supportive, and charming. They're good at handling difficult people or putting the right ones together, and they're especially effective in life when they're happily busy. Conversely, when they hit a slump, they can suddenly tip into passivity, looking to others to drive a situation or make key decisions. Chivvying serves no purpose and can make them worse. They just need backup, or peace, until the scales are rebalanced, or they may just need your undivided attention.

Trust that if your Libra Moon loved one says that they don't want to talk about it, they don't *mean* it. That is Libra speak for "I'm demotivated," "I'm upset," or "You don't understand." They'll settle in for a long listen when you need them, and they come back to life when they receive the same in return. For better or worse, friendship is their top priority.

Other Moon in Libra Celebrities

- Leo Sun: Iman
- Leo Sun: Meghan, Duchess of Sussex
- Virgo Sun: Agatha Christie
- Libra Sun: Kate Winslet
- Libra Sun: Sting
- Sagittarius Sun: Walt Disney
- Sagittarius Sun: Maria Callas
- Capricorn Sun: Bradley Cooper
- Capricorn Sun: Nicolas Cage
- Pisces Sun: Sidney Poitier

Moon in Scorpio

Element: Water

Mode: Fixed

Rulers: Mars & Pluto

Symbol: The Scorpion

Key phrase: I regenerate

Personality Traits

Scorpio is the Moon's sign of "fall," so it's a mismatch combination, but this doesn't automatically translate into bad news, unhappiness, or failure. Nevertheless, the journey to fulfillment or success is generally not an easy one for these deeply emotional individuals. The challenges that they face are invariably linked to the weighty Scorpio themes, yet these so often turn out to be the crux of their life story.

Who else could have done justice to Bram Stoker's *Dracula* or gangster movies like *The Godfather* series—a family saga of life, death, sex, power, and revenge—but Sun Aries, Moon Scorpio filmmaker Francis Ford Coppola? He contracted polio at the age of nine, which left him paralyzed for a year and a half. During his long recovery, he developed an interest in theatre and doing homemade productions. The rest, as they say, is history.

A Scorpio Moon can go into the Plutonic underworld and harrowing places that others would avoid. Coppola has company. Directors Alfred Hitchcock, Stanley Kubrick, Ridley Scott, and Steven Spielberg all have this awesome Moon. Their themes include innocent people in dangerous situations and depth psychology, but also the magical and mysterious. This is a witchy Moon that often indicates a fascination with the esoteric, a highly developed sixth sense, or even full-blown psychic powers. They're drawn to all that is connected to a deeper understanding of the human condition, from psychoanalysis to clairvoyance. This is the Moon of 16th century French astrologer, doctor, and seer, Nostradamus.

There's something about a Scorpio Moon that is somehow up close and personal with life and death issues, inextricably linked to courage, control, and survival. Early life-changing experiences can include a significant bereavement, illness, or—tragically common—emotional neglect or abuse. However, *never* write off Scorpio. It's through, and because of, pain or struggle that Scorpio Moon people discover their innate resilience, determination, and staying power.

Refusing to be beaten is a top hallmark but their Achilles heel is self-sabotage, hurting only themselves when resisting change for far too long. A Scorpio Moon's finest hours often lie in accepting endings. They excel at shedding an old skin, and reemerging as an upgraded version of their previous self.

In Relationships

The theme of consecutive signs working as opposites tells us a great deal about the nature and needs of this Moon. Partnership-oriented Libra naturally invites others into their world, but Scorpio can be an emotional fortress, fascinating but also extremely difficult to fathom.

First impressions of forcefulness, quiet strength, or even glacial silence can be intimidating, and are sometimes designed to be. Even when oozing their own particular brand of sexual magnetism, they can still keep others at arm's length. That's quite an achievement. A Scorpio Moon individual instinctively protects their own space while they privately get the measure of a new person or situation. When you're met with that piercing gaze, if only for a few seconds, you'll know that you're being put through the Scorpio screening.

It's crucial to clock that much of their behavior stems from needing to be the one in control. It isn't about any lack of feeling. On the contrary, as the Fixed

Water sign, Scorpio Moons embody the saying that still waters really do run deep. Under the surface is an intensely passionate nature that is teeming with life, in all its beauty and all its vulnerability, but they give nothing away. Tough early lessons in self-reliance can create complex trust issues. Many enter adult life seeking safety, such as being intent on having everything their own way or, at worst, battling addictions—substitutes for love.

If you're embarking on a relationship with a Moon in Scorpio person, romantic or professional, they can both intrigue and scare you, yet enrich your life beyond imagination. They don't do half-heartedness or indifference, only all or nothing, but you have to be patient, and real—they can see through fakery in a heartbeat. The golden rule of starting as you mean to go on applies more to this Moon than any other.

The first signs of insecurity with this Moon are jealousy or possessiveness. They then behave as if they own you, and can brood deeply on real or imagined hurts. They'll keep their own secrets, but they'll find out yours or accuse you of ones you don't have. Relationships in a tailspin can get vindictive and very messy. Don't underestimate them. Ever.

At best, these Moon people are super seductive, utterly devoted, and live life with great intensity. Everything matters, especially their partner, and they can do for better or worse, till death us do part, better than anyone.

Other Moon in Scorpio Celebrities

- Aries Sun: Lady Gaga
- Cancer Sun: Nelson Mandela
- Leo Sun: Ben Affleck
- Leo Sun: Jennifer Lopez
- Leo Sun: Matthew Perry
- Leo Sun: Roger Federer
- Virgo Sun: Beyoncé
- Libra Sun: Louise Hay
- Scorpio Sun: Katy Perry
- Capricorn Sun: Kate Moss

Moon in Sagittarius

Element: Fire

Mode: Mutable

Ruler: Jupiter

Symbol: The Archer

Key phrase: I seek

Personality Traits

After the intrigue, complexity, and mystery of Scorpio, we arrive in sunny Sagittarius. These Moon people have a naturally cheerful disposition, they're enthusiastic about life, and engage very easily with others of all ages and from all walks of life. They have the "ex" streak—exuberance, expansiveness, exaggeration, extravagance—and they're usually hard to miss. If there's a party going on, they're right in the middle of it, with that big smile and distinctive laugh.

This clownish streak is, however, very much their public face. Nobody can keep up that kind of feverish pace indefinitely and, as with all the Fire signs, their energy levels can drop without much warning. This can be due to anything from simply needing to recharge the batteries through to burnout. Either way, these individuals achieve much more in life when they learn how to pace themselves, to rest, and to practice self-care *before* the inevitable energy crash comes, rather than the other way around.

The tears of a clown apply to this Moon's private face. Essentially, they're born optimists, they can put a positive spin on just about anything, and their default setting is clever humor rather than doom and gloom. With Sagittarius as the sign of "the higher mind," these Moon people are philosophers and open books, until it comes to personal pain. Tears are shed alone, sometimes on the shoulder of someone who loves them unconditionally, but more usually in private. Not many people get to see the face behind the mask.

Possibly the most important need for this Moon is freedom, a theme that can show in a myriad of ways. Sometimes there's a nomadic childhood because of parents' work, such as moving frequently or living abroad. Or there's an innate restlessness that fuels a hunger for exploration, travel, and learning. Material security often gets delayed in the process, until they eventually find where they belong. It's not unusual for these Moon people to emigrate or to have a second home in another country. Spiritual writers Paulo Coelho and Kahlil Gibran both embody this Moon, with their global appeal—their bestsellers translated into 80–100 other languages—and settling away from their country of origin.

In Relationships

Those with a Sagittarius Moon tend to live life in a constant hurry, a haste that doesn't usually extend to the traditional settling down, especially in their younger years. These rolling stones are certainly not immune to love and romance, but the pull toward new experiences goes hand in hand with a resistance to making serious commitments. There's a built-in resentment toward being constrained, and too much early responsibility can kill their passion stone dead.

As the sign of the Archer, this Moon needs to fire their arrows and pursue them with zeal. They know how to have fun, which rubs off on those around them, so their ideal partner is a playmate, a traveling companion, or simply someone who shares their many interests or has plenty of their own. They respect intelligence and independence.

The Archer's zinging arrows also symbolize truth, justice, and faith. They need honesty and unconditional trust in all their close relationships, to the extent that this needs to be a total given. It's not in their own nature to be controlling or suspicious, but if there's real cause to start questioning a partner's fidelity, that is usually the emotional death knell for any kind of future.

Recovery for these Moon people, however, is not usually a long drawn-out process. Of all the Moon signs, even if they're brokenhearted, they are the least likely to turn cynical or embittered. In fact, many will keep their ex as a friend. They'll lick their wounds in private, learn from what went wrong, but eventually bounce back with that radiant red-carpet smile firmly in place. Apart from anything else, they find that being depressed is too boring. This Moon's saving grace is their appetite for a social life, their friends, and the next adventure. No matter how much they loved the ex, they love life more.

With the Sagittarius link to all things overseas, it's not at all unusual for these Moon people to find happiness with a partner from another culture. This was Rainier III, Prince of Monaco's Moon, whose marriage to American actress Grace Kelly made him a household name, while American actor Richard Gere's third marriage was to the love of his life, Spanish Alejandra Silva.

In many ways, this Moon is the full package. Highly entertaining and easygoing on one hand, deeply insightful and devoted on the other. When they love you, it's with every bit of their heart and soul. That's quite an act to follow.

Other Moon in Sagittarius Celebrities

- Taurus Sun: Adele
- Gemini Sun: Nicole Kidman
- Gemini Sun: Liam Neeson
- Libra Sun: Simon Cowell
- Scorpio Sun: Carl Sagan
- Capricorn Sun: Jeff Bezos
- Capricorn Sun: Anthony Hopkins
- Aquarius Sun: Oprah Winfrey
- Aquarius Sun: Jennifer Aniston
- Aquarius Sun: Yoko Ono

Moon in Capricorn

Element: Earth

Mode: Cardinal

Ruler: Saturn

Symbol: The Mountain Goat

Key phrase: I master

Personality Traits

The previous sign of Sagittarius is free-flowing, larger than life, and constantly on the move, so we start to understand Capricorn when we see the contrasting principles at work. These Moon people have a first response of stillness, holding back, and quietly assessing a person or a situation before they step into the arena. Even then, they will still take their time. Like their symbol of the Mountain Goat, they always watch where they're going, sure-footed and one eye on the summit. You can't rush this Moon—they set their own pace, staying within their own safety zones and boundaries.

However, first impressions of slowness can be misleading. They may take a long time to build self-confidence, but that doesn't stop them from dreaming big and quietly working on their plans and ideas. Capricorn has an ambitious streak a mile wide, usually has a definite goal in mind, and loves a project. These individuals are more determined than is at first obvious, sometimes even to themselves, and will persevere long after others would lose interest and fall by the wayside.

The Capricorn Moon's particular brand of ambition is nearly always linked to an unusual start in life, especially along the lines of having to grow up very quickly or missing out on childhood in other ways. Sometimes this is in response to poor parenting or because of losing a parent in their formative years. Conversely, the role model of a hardworking parent, or the active parental support of a child's special talents, are often significant factors in development. Either way, the concept of personal responsibility comes early, fostering self-reliance and an ability to be the adult in a situation. Sometimes these Moon people are simply old souls.

A deeply rooted sense of duty toward their own family or future generations is a strong hallmark of this Moon. This is environmental activist Greta Thunberg's Moon, the child who gave up waiting for the so-called grown-ups to sort out Mother Earth. Greta is also a wonderful example of how this Moon describes a nature that is so cool, yet perfectly capable of revealing impassioned beliefs or anger when needed.

In Relationships

The Moon is said to be in "detriment" in Capricorn, flagging up that this isn't the easiest of combinations. This doesn't mean that these individuals miss out on a love life, or that they lack lunar qualities such as nurturing and caring, but more that personal relationships are a serious matter. They're low on emotional risk-taking, high on building intimacy in their own gradual way, sometimes to the extent that their caution can easily be mistaken for indifference. Don't be fooled. Their own sensitivity is in there, but it's deeply buried treasure. Their ideal partnership is one that grows slowly, steadily, and very respectfully. Step by step. No cheating.

As with everything else in their life, these Moon people secretly see love as a project. Courteous, sexy, and utterly charming, it's easy for them to sow plenty of wild oats, but when it comes to true love and commitment, there are some very clear boxes to be ticked. Respectability matters. A partner doesn't have to be the traditional

pillar of society, although that certainly is often the case, but idlers and dreamers need not apply. Money matters, too, not for its own sake, but for the status that comes with someone who is hardworking, a high achiever, and self-sufficient. They find a lot of sex appeal in someone who others admire.

A significant difference in ages and/or finding the right partner later in life are both common themes with this Moon. Actor and film producer Michael Douglas was 53 when he met actress Catherine Zeta-Jones, exactly 25 years younger and who had just made her breakthrough into Hollywood. After strings of girlfriends, actor George Clooney was 52 when he found his soulmate in international human rights lawyer Amal, then 35.

Look for the humble streak. Those with a Capricorn Moon put themselves low down on the priority list while they do whatever they regard as their job, whether it's caring for family, building their own career, or championing a cause. Arguably their biggest need from a partner is support, not just in their daily routines and need to be organized but also in their duties and life choices.

Is it all work and seriousness? Far from it. Learning that they often struggle to say what they really mean or how they really feel is certainly a challenge, but behind every Capricorn Moon's privacy settings lie many delightful surprises. In particular, look no further for the best relationship gift of all—commitment wrapped up in a wonderfully witty and ironic sense of humor.

Other Moon in Capricorn Celebrities

- Aries Sun: Reese Witherspoon
- Aries Sun: Kate Hudson
- Taurus Sun: David Beckham
- Taurus Sun: Melania Trump
- Gemini Sun: Johnny Depp
- Libra Sun: Susan Sarandon
- Scorpio Sun: Indira Gandhi
- Sagittarius Sun: Brad Pitt
- Sagittarius Sun: Judi Dench
- Aquarius Sun: Charles Darwin
- Pisces Sun: Albert II, Prince of Monaco

Moon in Aquarius

Element: Air

Mode: Fixed

Rulers: Saturn & Uranus

Symbol: The Water Bearer

Key phrase: I understand

Personality Traits

If you want to practice the art of accepting others exactly as they are then your Moon in Aquarius person is the place to start. Quirky, clever, and unusual, these Moon people are a law unto themselves. You haven't got the faintest hope of ever being able to change them, but would you really want to? With their strong ethics, original minds, and awesome organizational skills, they have a great deal to offer, not just to their friends and family but also to their community, or even the world at large.

This is also the sign of groups and the collective, a hallmark that can show in all kinds of ways when expressed through the Moon. Diana, Princess of Wales, exemplified her Cancer Sun sign through the importance of children, family, and care, but it's in her humanitarian Aquarius Moon that we see the woman who revolutionized the old-fashioned British royal family and brought a whole new meaning to charity work. The People's (Aquarius) Princess (Moon) destigmatized AIDS, walked through minefields, and won hearts worldwide as she effortlessly pulled off that Aquarian feat of connecting with the public at a worldwide personal level.

Another hallmark of this Moon sign is above average intelligence, but not always of the academic kind, an especially important guideline with young children who show signs of brilliance or any kind of neurodiversity. Different is not disordered. Going into adulthood, their business acumen, strong political beliefs, or a hunger for knowledge and new experiences all contribute to these Moon people's own special way of standing out in the crowd.

These individuals usually know, many from a very early age, that they have some kind of "differentness" about them and often break out of their family molds. This reflects the New Age Aquarius links to innovators, trendsetters, rebels, or reformers, in their daily lives or life's purpose.

In real life, American actress and model Marilyn Monroe was far from being the "dumb blonde" that the studios promoted. She was a voracious reader with a personal library of hundreds of books, started her own production company at the age of 29, and made her mark as a civil rights activist.

In Relationships

Aquarius is arguably the most complex of all the Moon signs when it comes to understanding their emotional makeup. They can have difficulty making sense of it themselves. Often this can be traced back to a tough start in life, when circumstances didn't allow for much love and warmth of the nurturing kind. This can be anything on the scale from an unusual upbringing, through to early hardship or broken homes. Either way, these Moon people generally enter the romance arena with either naive, disconnected, or unconventional ideas about relationships.

In terms of first impressions, this Moon is a cool customer. Their opposite sign of fiery Leo does everything with visible passion and easily attracts attention, but an Aquarius Moon needs to test out a new situation or person before allowing any kind

of intimacy. Everything starts with understanding, and a checklist. Their ideal romance springs from friendship, and their biggest turn-on is a true meeting of minds. Tick!

These Moon people care deeply about principles and injustice in the world, which extends to their personal relationships, too. They have a very clear sense of what they perceive to be right or wrong and they're not afraid to speak their mind. If they think that you've said or done anything that is, to them, unfair or ethically dubious, they will tell you so. In no uncertain terms.

It's not easy being on the receiving end of this Moon's strong opinions but, to them, it's actually an expression of love. They speak out in the spirit of wanting what is best and right—for you and for them—not to pick a fight. They won't drop you. They'll pull away only if someone is beyond their understanding or, more usually, they won't develop that relationship in the first place. They have an analytical and objective streak that enables them to detach from anything that they find uncomfortable, immoral, or ridiculous, rather than wasting their time.

At home, they need tolerance—a flexible family or partner who gives them plenty of space, and simply accepts their methodical and systematic ways of doing things. They're allergic to being controlled, or to being used as a sounding board for problems that never change or ideas that never happen. Expect the brisk brush-off, not a sympathetic ear! When you genuinely need them, however, these Moon people are right there. They thrive on those moments of knowing that you're each other's best friend.

Other Moon in Aquarius Celebrities

- Aries Sun: Russell Crowe
- Aries Sun: Victoria Beckham
- Gemini Sun: Morgan Freeman
- Leo Sun: Helen Mirren
- Libra Sun: John Lennon
- Sagittarius Sun: Britney Spears
- Sagittarius Sun: Pope Francis
- Capricorn Sun: Diane Keaton
- Aquarius Sun: Princess Stéphanie of Monaco
- Pisces Sun: Glenn Close

Moon in Pisces

Element: Water

Mode: Mutable

Rulers: Jupiter & Neptune

Symbol: The Fishes

Key phrase: I redeem

Personality Traits

Following on from the methodical, rational, and logical world of Aquarius, we arrive in supersensitive Pisces, who operates solely on feelings and instincts. Their opposite number of Virgo, a "mind sign," makes sense of the world through thought and analysis. For soulful Pisces, however, everything comes down to how something, or someone, makes them feel.

The symbolism of Neptune, god of the seas, reflects the essential Piscean qualities—dreamy, boundless, and often unfathomable. These Moon people are full of emotional or magical mysteries and take a great deal of getting to know. They have hidden depths and a "handle with care" wrapper. They rarely have an easy start in life and can be affected deeply if they suffered at the hands of adults who demanded too much, or who failed to recognize the child's fragility.

Water takes only the shape of the vessel, so those with a Pisces Moon learn from an early age to pour themselves into any mold, especially if they're trying to fit in or please others. This fluidity defines the struggle to find their personal sense of self, but it's also an indication of empathy, a special gift, or remarkable creative talent—something that is simply innate and could never be taught. Geniuses Leonardo da Vinci and Michelangelo are both on this list, along with a number of exceptional musicians and actors. Back in the golden heyday of the movies, we find actresses Audrey Hepburn, Rita Hayworth, Ava Gardner, and Grace Kelly all with this mesmerizing Moon.

However, without support, healing work, or very high self-awareness, these Moon people can self-sabotage. They're especially at risk of using addiction to disconnect from their insecurities or too much reality. Ava Gardner and Rita Hayworth both engaged in alcohol misuse, while singers Elvis Presley, Michael Jackson, and Prince all famously died from drug misuse.

The biggest challenge for those born under this Moon is to keep their dreams alive, but to foster an inner strength of serenity, rather than constantly being at the mercy of a tough world. Only then can they truly prosper from their awesome creative and imaginative talents.

In Relationships

In the process of learning life's lessons while protecting the sanctum of their inner world, this "all at sea" Moon needs an anchor, especially in the shape of those who are consistently supportive. This is easier said than done. These Moon people can be very impressionable, easily attracting chaotic or needy people, or narcissists who latch onto their empathic nature. Falling in love is all too often hampered by the Pisces tendency to idealize, and then to be devastated when the unrealistic romance falls apart.

Audrey Hepburn married twice, had many on-set affairs, and then a third long-term partner for the last 13 years of her life. Her rock, however, was fashion designer

Hubert de Givenchy. They had a deep and mutual personal attachment for 40 years and he described the bond as "a kind of marriage."

Pisces Moon people have a vulnerability that leaves them wide open to other people's careless words or behavior. They cry easily, especially when they come up against their demons of disillusionment, self-pity, or, at worst, paranoia. If you want to build an authentic relationship with a Pisces Moon person, then guard against any kind of harsh criticism and never promise what cannot be delivered. They seek fusion but, in fact, need firm, clear, and loving boundaries, and gentleness above all else.

When hurt, they stumble at putting feelings into words. Explanations don't come easily at the time, and they can simply fall mute. However, this doesn't mean that the emotional minefield is suddenly a safe zone or that the reactions aren't happening. They're simply in overwhelm, insights take shape gradually, but when they "just know" something in their own hearts they can be unshakeable. Sometimes the silence can be deliberate or manipulative, because they can be either rescuer or victim. They're not above the occasional "sad not mad," or sweet-talking you when they want something.

When it comes to pure love, these Moon people are the zodiac's jackpot. They feel everything in glorious technicolor, and it can be rather wonderful to be in their fairy tale. They'll believe in you with all their heart. Throughout their 55-year marriage, author J. R. R. Tolkien wrote love poems to his wife and made his name and fortune through his "high fantasy" works, including *The Lord of the Rings*.

Other Moon in Pisces Celebrities

- Cancer Sun: Robin Williams
- Leo Sun: Coco Chanel
- Leo Sun: Matt LeBlanc
- Leo Sun: Robert De Niro
- Leo Sun: Robert Plant
- Libra Sun: Catherine Zeta-Jones
- Scorpio Sun: Hillary Clinton
- Sagittarius Sun: Frank Sinatra
- Aquarius Sun: Paul Newman
- Pisces Sun: Martin Scorsese

Chapter Two

Moon Watching

The Moon travels through all 12 zodiac signs each month, with a cycle of approximately 29 days, meaning she changes sign roughly every 2½ days. Observing this journey and seeing how the symbolism of each sign plays out in our daily lives can teach us a great deal about the workings of the zodiac.

Living in Tune With the Moon

We can, of course, actively and consciously choose particular Moon days as "the best day" to do the things related to that sign, and in that sense the Moon's journey through the signs provides us with an excellent tour guide. However, even more interestingly, when we engage in careful Moon watching, we find more often than not that the matters connected to each sign are naturally at the top of the pile. Here are some examples from my own life.

- When I decided that my kitchen needed a really deep spring-clean, I contacted professional cleaners to do the job. They were very busy but gave me their next available appointment, which I accepted straightaway. I *then* looked in the Ephemerides (see page 140) and smiled to see that the Moon would be moving into Virgo (the sign of health, hygiene, perfectionism, and attention to detail) on that morning. On the day, every cupboard was emptied and cleaned, every item was washed, no shelf or corner left untouched, and then everything restored to its original position. When I posted a picture on Facebook, friends asked if I'd had a new kitchen put in. It was gleaming and worth every single euro.
- When I contacted a new accountant, again, I simply accepted the first appointment offered to me, which was a couple of weeks' wait. When that date approached, I was very busy and considered postponing the appointment, but checked in with the Moon first. The time scheduled for meeting with the accountant put the Moon at the very beginning of Taurus (the sign of money and safety). The message was clear. Don't cancel, find the time. I did, and she was of invaluable help. I came away with information that was completely new to me and important in terms of my post-Brexit security here in Greece, home for the last 30 years.
- When I asked my friend, colleague, and fellow author Elisabeth Brooke to be my official reader for this book—which means being the first person to read my text, both for literary criticism and astrological accuracy—I noted the time of the conversation. It was a perfect showing. The Moon (women) was at 0 degrees (beginnings) of Capricorn (business, career, professionalism, status).

I love these kinds of examples because they illustrate the crucial point about how astrology really works. We are reminded again and again that astrology is not "causal," at a natal or a predictive level. Our natal Moon sign (see Chapter 2) doesn't *make* us a certain way, it shows us that we *are* a certain way, which is slightly different. The same rule applies to daily astrology. The journey of the Moon and the other planets through the signs do not *make* things happen, they show us what *is* happening, so it's all about looking through the other end of the telescope.

None of my examples were consciously chosen, but the timing simply confirmed that I was in step with the universe. In some magical and unknowable way, the heavens work in an "as above, so below" way, reflecting back to us our life on planet Earth. This leads us on from everyone's first question—does astrology work?—to the infinitely more fascinating question—how come it works? There's no one single clear answer to that, but it doesn't take long to discover that we are undoubtedly connected. Learning how to look into that vast celestial mirror, and to interpret that which is being reflected back to us, is the essence of astrological work.

Early and Late Degrees

As the Moon has a cycle of roughly 29 days, she changes sign roughly every 2½ days. In other words, she will move from 0 degrees to 30 degrees of each sign in the space of about 60 hours. 0 degrees is potent, for any planet or the Moon, as this is the moment of marking the very beginning of a new journey. So, whenever you get the chance, pay very close attention to unfolding events, your feelings, ideas, or the things that simply present themselves every time the Moon changes sign.

Similarly, I've definitely noticed that the latter degrees of a sign can be troublesome. These are when matters are more likely to become complex, frustrating, time-consuming, or even pointless. This fits perfectly with the teachings of traditional astrology, which names 0 and 29 as "critical degrees." This doesn't mean critical as in a crisis, although that can sometimes be the case, but more as in sensitized. When it comes to Moon watching, simply think of 0 as beginnings and 29 as endings, and observe how matters start, how they move on, and how they gradually reach their conclusions.

When the Moon is in Aries

Element: Fire

Mode: Cardinal

Ruler: Mars

Symbol: The Ram

Embrace New Beginnings

Aries correlates to the 1st House of the zodiac where we locate everything to do with the unfettered self, ego, and personal image. If you want to make any kind of fresh start in terms of your diet, fitness, wardrobe, or general appearance, then the Moon's arrival in Aries is the starting gun. It's also the perfect time to get a new project up and running or to revitalize the things that have been neglected.

Look at the tasks and issues in your life that, with a little bit of refreshed effort, could come good. It may even be a big time-saver to start again from scratch. Equally, if something has been going wrong, don't be afraid to write it off. Either way, you'll be looking through fresh and wide-open eyes.

Remember that when the Sun arrives at 0 degrees of Aries every March, that's the moment of the Spring Equinox—the astrological New Year—so there's a monthly dose of exactly the same kind of spring fever to tap into. Draw a line under anything that has already taken up far too much time and energy. Distance the people who drain you and especially the ones who tend to criticize you. The power of self-belief is rocket fuel, no matter what anyone else says. The Aries answer to "you can't" is "watch me." Back yourself. Make your resolutions.

Take Action

Make it a golden rule that if you want something doing, do it yourself if possible—try not to be overly, or remotely, reliant on other people. The Aries Moon is fantastic for getting things moving, so go the most direct route. Aries loves a straight line from A to B, no messing. In your business dealings, avoid the dreaded "death by email" trap and pick up the phone. Go straight to the person you need to talk to or straight to the top.

Aries thrives on firsts, fresh starts, and taking the initiative. Fight back where you need to, but don't be angry or go leading the uprising just for the sake of it. Appropriate anger means having a real cause. Aries loves a mission, with defending the underdog at the top of the list. The warrior spirit can light a fire in our belly and produce quick, sometimes instant, results.

On an emotional level, these Aries days are designed for shaking off hurts or grievances, for waking up to the fact that letting go frees up our vital energy that can be so much better used elsewhere. Don't forget that the best revenge is to build a fantastic life.

Champion Yourself

We've come to use the word "selfish" in a pejorative way, in the sense of describing someone who is unable to put anyone else first, but the true Aries energy is about being "self"-ish in a proactive way. These Aries days are about looking after ourselves and focusing on what can be called healthy narcissism. It's akin to why you should put on your own oxygen mask first, which is about both personal survival *and* about being of use to another person. The two are inextricably linked because we're of no use to anyone else if we're always in a mess. Or unconscious.

Building a powerful love affair with ourselves is something that most of us find very difficult to do, especially earlier on in life when we're at our most vulnerable. Entering the minefield of adult life is hard enough, but without the protection of healthy self-esteem, it's a real war zone. Aries days remind us that this armor is still available to us; that self-love can be an acquired skill and one that needs constant practice.

Protect your ego—we all have one—and don't be afraid of being alone, in every sense of the word. Single or partnered, we're all on our own individual journey. Embracing the power of independence, maintaining healthy boundaries in our personal relationships, decision-making, and achieving without the need for constant external validation—these are the kind of empowering Aries hallmarks to look out for and to put into practice as every monthly lunar cycle begins.

How to Relax

The danger with this Moon is burnout. Fast and furious is a great pace to set for being a high achiever, but it's vital to recharge the batteries. Chill. There's nothing that can't wait until the next morning.

What to Wear

There's only one color for Aries and that's red—the brighter, the better. Also consider wearing anything sharp and slick, especially if you want to stand out from the crowd.

When the Moon is in Taurus

Element: Earth

Mode: Fixed

Ruler: Venus

Symbol: The Bull

Get Grounded

We can approach this monthly lunar journey through the zodiac by remembering that consecutive signs work, to a large extent, as opposites. While Aries blazes a trail, Taurus slows us down. As Aries rules the self, both our ego and the physical body, it follows then that earthy Taurus rules sustenance, how we find the resources to care for the body in terms of survival, and how we go about our modern-day foraging.

The Moon is said to be "exalted" in Taurus, so it's her top sign. This makes sense when we consider that Taurus is all about the five senses, showing that we're physically connected to planet Earth through what we can see, hear, smell, touch, and taste. After the supercharged, but sometimes frenetic, couple of Aries days, the message now is to take stock and get grounded.

Focus on Your Food

With the Moon's links to home and nurture, these Taurus days are perfect for channeling your inner domestic goddess. Starting by taking control of everything on the food front is a top box to tick for this Moon and is an instant remedy for feeling better about ourselves. Clean out the fridge, hit the supermarkets or order in, cook for the freezer, or cook for others. Moon in Taurus days are perfect for gathering friends or family around your kitchen table, or eating out for a social occasion. Your chances of having a bad meal are much lower.

As well as enjoying culinary delights, it also helps to remember that food is medicine as well as fuel and pleasure. We are what we eat, so stop and think about your diet and what fills up your supermarket trolley. How much of it might be classed as junk? Do you suffer from "food noise?" Taurus' planet Venus rules all that is sweet and loves sugar, so be aware of comfort eating or wobbly blood sugar levels. Whether we want to eat more healthily, lose weight, or go completely organic, this time of the month is a dig in the ribs about our relationship with food.

Consider Your Finances

As the sign of resources, it follows that Taurus links directly to money, primarily our personal earning power and our appreciation of the things that money can buy. Watch out for more focus, for good or ill, on income, bill paying, possessions, all material goods, and life's luxuries.

It's one of life's truisms that when we have money, we never think about it, but when we haven't got it, we can't think about anything else. One of the most important things that Moon in Taurus loves and needs is security, so if there are financial issues to address, then these Taurus days are heaven sent for finding answers or help, whether we're on the giving or receiving end. Seek professional financial advice if needed.

If there's money to spare, then enjoy it. A warning bell, however, is that Taurus loves retail therapy but can definitely be overly acquisitive. Be careful not to end up with a lot more "stuff" that you really don't need or which could quickly lose its appeal and feel like waste. Watch out for any addictive tendencies and question them. What are they really about? Just as food can be comfort eating, shopping can also be a way of filling a hole. What's the real need? The answer to that question is always love, but with Taurus it's often about feeling safe and protected, too.

Money is energy, so keep it moving. Offer to pay for something; it will mean more to the other person than you might imagine. If it's the other way around, then your job is simply to accept generosity with good grace and appreciation. Crucially, be aware of the connection between cost and value, and think about what your money is really buying. A cab instead of public transport might seem like extravagance but we're often buying time or safety. I once cleaned out what was left in my bank account to take my beloved sister out for lunch after her purse was stolen. I wasn't really buying food, I was supplying love, comfort, and support. I never regretted it. My sister never forgot it. More work immediately came my way.

How to Relax

Connect with nature—walking, gardening, visiting parks and the countryside. Anything tactile or sensual, from home beautifying to salon treatments such as Reiki, massage, a body scrub, or a facial.

What to Wear

There are two extremes for Taurus—pure glamour for going out or, for staying in, it's your tat, or your oldest, comfiest sofa pajamas.

When the Moon is in Gemini

Element: Air

Mode: Mutable

Ruler: Mercury

Symbol: The Twins

Engage With the World

Gemini correlates to the 3rd House of the zodiac where we locate everything that sits under that huge umbrella called "communication and transport," fittingly ruled by Mercury, the Winged Messenger. It comes as no surprise, then, to find that these fidgety Gemini days are among the busiest of the month and, after the stillness and sustenance of Taurus, the mood can jump to positively frenetic.

Catching up with friends and family—plenty of chats on the phone or messaging, exchanging news and the latest gossip—sharing on social media, learning about things that interest you, putting people in touch with others, or traveling within your locale to see friends, spontaneously or for planned events—these are the kind of things to expect under a restless and curious Gemini Moon.

It isn't just people on the move either. News travels fast on these days so spread the word while the grapevine is humming, but factor in that the rumor mills will be grinding away, too, so don't believe everything you hear. This Moon is a must for fact-checking and, if you want something to stay private, then definitely keep it under wraps.

Multitask–But Don't Overdo It

You would think that the Moon in Gemini time of the month would be ideal for writing or any kind of creative work but, in my experience, this is not always the case. The sign of Mutable Air is known for a butterfly mind, flitting from one thing to the next, learning a little about a lot, so these Gemini days tend to be the ones where we're more easily distracted or simply spinning a lot of other plates. Take extra care with work that needs total accuracy, or with PINs and passwords.

As the sign of the Twins rules duality, or very often multiplicity, too, it certainly follows that these are ideal multitasking days. However, Gemini rules the nervous system, so too much hyperactivity isn't a great idea. Get plenty of sleep so that you can tackle a to-do list with fresh energy, delegate where necessary, and especially find helping hands for the jobs that are beyond your own area of expertise.

That's on a good day. On a bad day, the flip side of this Moon's coin is being in overwhelm and having no headspace. Being overly preoccupied makes it a tall order to think straight. Too much else going on, too many people wanting our attention, losing time through tasks or demands that we hadn't expected—these are the kind of time bandits that can make Gemini hours slip through our fingers. This all adds up to scrambled thoughts or constant interruption, the death knell for things like studying, writing, or creativity, all of which require solitude and intense concentration.

Feel Inspired

In terms of cashing in on the Gemini love of both the written and spoken word, think starting points. Gemini is the first Air sign of the zodiac so these are among the best days for being inventive, for developing our ideas, or coming up with new ones. In fact, pay close attention to those inspired moments and don't let your brainwaves slip the net. You can develop the details later.

At work, listen to younger voices and schedule meetings or brainstorming when everyone is more likely to be quick thinking and receptive to different ways of doing things. Perception of choice—that "spirits lifting" moment when we realize that there are other options—is the top psychological gift of this Moon. Gemini is the expert at not being cornered.

On the same theme, someone may be impossible to pin down, or avoiding us. Leave them be. Focus on your present and significant relationships. These days lend themselves to real connection, more so than the emotional Water signs. Putting feelings into words can bring clarity on both sides, as long as it doesn't get too heavy. That's when defensive "two versions" Gemini lies get told. Keep the best of Gemini's light touch in mind—breaking the ice, making someone laugh, clever solution finding, and the gift of quick results, personally or professionally.

If you're out shopping, for anything, this Moon is a gift for the bargains. How often have we mourned the demise of a favorite item? If you find something you absolutely love, buy two. Selling something? List it in two different places, not just one.

How to Relax

Slow down. You can't be all things to all people, or in two places at the same time. Create some "me time." Fresh air is also a must, especially for keeping a clear head.

What to Wear

Wake up your wardrobe. Revive anything faded with a dye; try anything vibrant or multicolored or with spots or stripes. Also try combinations of something old, something new—mix it up.

When the Moon is in Cancer

Element: Water

Mode: Cardinal

Ruler: The Moon

Symbol: The Crab

Prioritize Your Homelife

This sign correlates to the 4th House of the zodiac where we locate everything to do with our roots and family, home and property. After the animated interactions and constant circulation of Gemini, we now return to stillness, to our private world, which allows us space and time for some introspection. While Gemini is all about being "out there," Cancer is the sign of "in here," behind the closed doors of our own sanctuary, in the realms of our domestic life and inner thoughts.

As Mother Moon symbolizes all that is connected to procreation, parenting, and homemaking, it makes perfect sense that she rules Cancer, her only sign of "dignity." There is a clear and natural synergy between the sign and the planet. However, this doesn't automatically mean that Moon in Cancer days are housebound or that homelife turns into an idyll. On the contrary, it's more usually a case of tending to that machinery that keeps everything running.

On an emotional level, Cancer's role of nurturing, protecting, and holding can work beautifully in our favor when it comes to being there for those who need us, and vice versa. This especially applies to family, our clan, but also to those in our community who look out for us. Those who come to our rescue as the Moon arrives in Cancer are usually conspicuous by their presence.

Themes of care intensify hugely at times of illness, especially with regard to children or the elderly. Moon in Cancer days will highlight these kinds of concerns, along with the division of labor among family members. From housework to childcare, gardening to dog walking, who does what? Look out for martyrdom.

If income allows, these days are ideal for employing others to help out and free up your time. All labor-saving devices get the green light, too, as do security issues. From smoke or burglar alarms to the paperwork of pensions, insurance, resident permits, or tax returns—get list-ticking.

Unhook–Physically and Emotionally

Cancer can be a hoarder. We all have drawers, cabinets, or closets that seem to gather junk when we're not looking, but if you have serious clutter then get ruthless. These Moon in Cancer days are ideal for getting the message about letting go of the things that we don't need, or even want, and which are simply taking up space. Destination: the trash can or thrift/charity shops. Conversely, choose these days to go secondhand store shopping. Your chances of finding the bargains, objects of beauty for your home, or even genuine antiques are considerably higher.

We all attach great value to where we live. Whether it be a mansion or a room, it's home sweet home, and this Moon extends to all property concerns, including buying, selling, or looking for somewhere to rent. The Moon's arrival in her own sign is an especially powerful moment, so aim to "go live" with your hunting or advertising as the Moon clicks into Cancer, and watch the time wasters drop away.

Emotional baggage also shuffles its way to the top of the pile. This Moon reminds us of the importance of unhooking from the past so that, in the present, we don't hurt those who didn't wound us. Similarly, it's not in our interests to cling to the wreckage of any relationship that will never be healthy, no matter what we invest in it. A Cancer Moon includes self-care, retreating into our protective shell when necessary, rather than thinking that everything has to be rescued.

The previous sign of Gemini can talk its way out of any corner, but when the Moon is in Cancer there's a case to be made for some avoidance when, all of a sudden, everyone seems to be so touchy or bearing grudges. Approach sensitive issues side-on, or take control tactfully, quietly, and subtly. On that point, this is a great Moon for secrecy in a caring capacity, too, such as planning surprise parties or ordering specially chosen gifts that will take a long while to arrive. Cancerian issues can often relate to the longer term rather than immediacy.

There's a brilliant business streak to this sign, too, so choose these days for working from home or even for starting your own company. The Cancer tenacity succeeds where other signs give up.

How to Relax

Are you being oversensitive? Consciously unhook from grievances, and breathe. Be wherever and with whomever brings you the most peace.

What to Wear

Think moonlight on the water. Go for white, silvers, or soft blues in cashmere or silk. At home, this is the Moon for old favorites; the things that you'll never throw away.

When the Moon is in Leo

Element: Fire

Mode: Fixed

Ruler: The Sun

Symbol: The Lion

Be Bold

This sign correlates to the 5th House of the zodiac, which is often referred to as the fun zone. It's here that we locate our creativity, our passion, lovers, and our love of life itself. Little wonder then that this is the House of children, those whom we create but also those who spark up our fiercest love and protective instincts. Think lioness watching over her cubs. When the Moon is in Leo, we can expect to be more involved with or concerned for our youngsters or anyone who's the center of our world, the ones for whom we'd crawl over hot coals.

In sharp contrast to the previous sign of home-based and cautious Cancer, these Leo days tend to bring us out of hiding, moving from understated to overstated. Success at work may link directly to getting ourselves noticed, including blowing our own trumpet if we have to, so don't be modest. Leo brings out our sense of entitlement, and calls on our courage and confidence. Why shouldn't we have our five minutes of fame? Give praise where praise is due, but accept it, too.

Know Your Worth

The Leo Moon reminds us that moving up the professional ladder or finding real job satisfaction is inextricably tied up with knowing our worth. Leo is definitely not designed to be a small cog in a big wheel and this Moon has a way of bringing that message home to us, sometimes through dealing with those who are highly regarded, someone that others look up to. Observe them closely. How do they operate? Do they have work habits or some kind of personal touch that picks them out as top cat? The Leo Moon is fabulous for learning from those who are excellent role models.

Any situation in which we're underpaid or unappreciated, in our working or personal lives, can be much harder to bear under Leo skies, but that's the whole point. Dissatisfaction—that moment when we absolutely know that we deserve better—is a powerful catalyst for real change. Hand in hand with the Leo creativity is vision, the ability to picture something that we know is both inspired and achievable, even if others doubt or mock. Don't look for approval. The only person you need to impress is yourself.

Connect With Others

This is also the Moon of the drama queen, so don't exhaust the goodwill or patience of those around you. While we may be busy channeling our inner royalty, everything always works both ways, so show your appreciation to others and don't take anyone or anything for granted. You may also find that you're using up favors fast so be super selective and manage your expectations. Asking the right person to do the right thing at the right time can make a huge difference, so be aware of others' strengths, and weaknesses.

At the heart of Leo symbolism is efficiency, organizational skills, and getting away with being bossy. Whether it's supporting others at work, managing complaints, or throwing a party, this Moon thrives on playing a central role in bringing others together and making positive events happen. This is arguably the best Moon for entertaining if you're planning a special event, especially at home—houseproud, lavish, warm, and welcoming, and a way of making all that hard work look oh so easy.

Treat Yourself

This is a generous Moon that knows all about the importance of pleasure. There's nothing wrong with some pure extravagance, whether it's something special just for you or which includes others who matter to you. Try not to think just in terms of how much things cost. In fact, when acting on something heartfelt, watch how the money usually follows. These Leo days are heaven sent for restoring our belief in abundance, whether we're on the giving or receiving end.

Leo-Moon days are not designed for doing anything on the cheap and it's worth paying for the best. Hair appointments—tending to the lion's mane—are a top example. I'll never forget going to a famous London salon on the day of a Leo New Moon and every single chair was taken by a woman with long blond hair having her sun-kissed highlights done.

Last word to the felines—special treats or needs may extend to your cat. You can find a wonderful vet, or you'll hear of animal rescue work. This is the top Moon for adopting from a sanctuary.

How to Relax

In a word, pampering. Spa days are purr-fect for this Moon and are well worth saving up for. At home, the lion's den is all about comfort and plenty of sleep.

What to Wear

The Sun's sign points to yellow, gold, orange, and, of course, animal print. Wear anything eye-catching, not forgetting quality, statement jewelry, for an unforgettable first impression.

When the Moon is in Virgo

Element: Earth

Mode: Mutable

Ruler: Mercury

Symbol: The Maiden

Face Challenges Head-On

Virgo correlates to the 6th House of the zodiac where we locate everything to do with our day-to-day working lives. This encompasses everything from the jobs we do to make ends meet through to our particular interests, natural talents, and acquired skills. This is Mercury's feminine sign, his masculine sign being Gemini, so again, we see themes of quick and clever brainwork, but definitely more in the shape of analysis, a marked attention to detail, and the art of problem-solving.

In fact, as the Moon arrives in Virgo, it's not uncommon for things to start going wrong. Often there's some kind of challenge that requires our close attention and which usually doesn't have an immediately obvious answer. Coming up against something that creates extra work for ourselves or someone else, making or discovering mistakes, needing help in the shape of someone else's expertise, a duty that we can't get out of—these are the kind of themes to look out for as the Virgo Moon puts both our abilities and our patience to the test. We just have to roll up our shirt sleeves and get on with it.

Be Proactive

Virgo and the 6th House are also in charge of everything to do with our health—physical and mental. Make those appointments—especially if you're worried about something—for yourself, a loved one, or a pet, because the 6th House is where we locate all small animals.

This can be a fretful Moon so we need to soothe our anxieties, not feed them. We can also be more sensitive to criticism, including beating ourselves up. The thing that's going round and round in your mind, try to let yourself off that obsessive hook. If it's something in your procrastination box then move it to the top of your to-do list and action it.

If it's something personal or emotional, again, try to deal with it straightaway. For anything that's genuinely out of your control then the watchword is acceptance. It is what it is. You can keep picking it apart but it won't make any difference. It will be sorted when the time is right. In the meantime, if we can't change the problem, remember that we can always change our attitude to it. The payoffs of this Moon include learning curves, job satisfaction, or being of invaluable service to someone who needs you in particular, or your expertise in general.

Deal With the Details—But Don't Forget to Relax, Too

Virgo makes us work, physically and mentally, and loves to throw brainteasers or fiddly jobs into the mix that can be time-consuming and tiresome at the time, but ultimately satisfying. The things we learn under a Virgo Moon tend to be things we'll use again and again in our lives or are lessons that don't need to be learned twice.

Similarly, effort invested in sorting out the paraphernalia of life can save us a lot of hassle in the long run, with admin high up on the list. Fill in those forms, especially for job applications or insurance, and don't forget to read the small print. In fact, a golden rule with this Moon is to do nothing in a rush, and to assume nothing. Virgo is nothing if not meticulous, so double-checking and fact-checking both get huge ticks. Sweat the small stuff.

Decluttering in every sense is definitely therapy for this Moon and this extends to your home. Get on top of the housework, throw out the junk, and find a place for the things that are taking up table or worktop space. Virgo is the expert at stripping things back to basics and is associated with frugality, but also with quality. Clever economizing works well under this Moon as long as it's not triggered by meanness, which usually backfires on us. Focus on value for money in the spirit of spending your cash wisely, not wastefully.

So Virgo is all work and no play, right? Wrong! That's definitely one of those astrological myths that doesn't take long to dismantle. There's something about this demanding Moon that tells us when we need to let our hair down or simply unwind, alone or with our favorite people. Very often, it's the latter. Let's not forget that this is a Mercury sign, who is all about communication not isolation, with humor and conversation as the talking cure.

How to Relax

Know when to say "good enough," and stop. Also tap into the perfect combination of Virgo discipline and gentleness for all mind-body-spirit practices, such as yoga or tai chi.

What to Wear

When it matters, such as for meetings or interviews, go for the immaculately put together look that Virgo does so well. When you're off duty, think understated, easy-to-wear, and natural fabrics.

When the Moon is in Libra

Element: Air

Mode: Cardinal

Ruler: Venus

Symbol: The Scales

Consider Your Partner–Personal or Professional

As we arrive at the halfway point of the zodiac, we can start to think in terms of opposites. So, Aries as the first sign is all about the individual, our sense of self and personal desires, how we accomplish things and grow into our independence. The opposite sign of Libra correlates to the 7th House of the zodiac, which is where we locate our significant other, personal or professional, where we are dependent on another, and how we interact on a one-to-one basis.

We're all familiar with the idea that the sign of the Scales is famous for indecision and weighing things up, but it's also the sign of partnership. The slightest touch on one side of the scales equally affects the other, thus what one person does automatically affects the other. On the love front, Libra is all about relating and togetherness, so these days of the month are perfect for meeting someone new, getting back into the dating scene or for "date nights" with your partner.

We're also reminded that what may be a priority for us isn't necessarily a priority for another. Or something that we'd happily spend money on would be considered a waste of money by someone else. Sound familiar? This is a top area of dispute in partnerships—who spends how much on what—so don't forget that Venus rules the cash as well as love.

Seek Company From Others

The Moon tells us what is needed and in Libra that means involving "the other," whether this is partner, family, friend, or colleague. These days are ideal for arranging to do things with someone else rather than going it alone, either because you like this person's company and having them with you will simply make things more enjoyable, or because you'll benefit from someone else's advice or opinions. Two heads really are better than one.

If you're in overwhelm, if you need specific help, or just another pair of hands, the message is that "you're not alone," even if you feel as though you are. The time is right to ask someone to do something for you, either as a favor or as a paid job. Often, this is something that is actually easy for another person to do, they just need to be asked and will be only too happy to help. Conversely, we may find ourselves doing all kinds of things for other people, and feeling the appreciation.

Moon-Libra days are not designed for keeping things to ourselves—they are a gift for discovering the art of delegation, collaboration, or brainstorming. Bounce your thoughts or ideas off another person and pay close attention to how this brings answers to the surface. Words that had been floating around in the back of your mind suddenly take shape and rearrange themselves into cohesive sentences. Or chance comments in a conversation can throw you a great idea or solution to an issue that will save you time, money, or angst. If you simply need to vent and get feeling into words, then choose a good listener. Expect close friends to seek you out in the same way.

Come to Decisions and Agreements

Listen out for words like "I have to make a big decision" or "I don't know what to do." In such statements, we hear the famous Libran indecision and the talking cure is needed. Just clock, though, that one of the pitfalls of this Moon is that she can be a time bandit—we're not dealing with the stuff of quick answers or snap decisions, but with investigating all the options and possibilities. Set boundaries and steer the conversation toward solution finding, especially when you need to arrive at agreements that work for both sides.

One of the most important Libran messages is that the relationships really worth having, in our personal and professional lives, are negotiated ones. Encourage effective communication, compromise, and cooperation, all done in that "gently, gently" way, and get tough with one person laying down the law. If you need someone's blessing, or permission, Libra-Moon days are a good choice.

Libra and Venus rule the pursuit of peace. On May 8, 2025, when the news broke that the world had a new Pope, the Moon was in the early degrees of Libra, unanimous agreement had been reached, and Pope Leo XIV's opening words as he arrived on the balcony were "Peace be with all of you."

How to Relax

Venus-ruled Libra makes for a beautifying Moon. Go for one-to-one salon treatments—the partnership of beauty therapist and client. Libra-Moon evenings are perfect for social events or catching up with friends.

What to Wear

Libra has powerful links to the world of fashion, style, and design. Go for anything coordinated and chic, and in the colors that suit you.

When the Moon is in Scorpio

Element: Water

Mode: Fixed

Rulers: Mars & Pluto

Symbol: The Scorpion

Connect With Your Spirituality

The second sign of Taurus is all about the earthy and sensual world, all that is visible and knowable. The opposite sign of Scorpio therefore rules all that is invisible and unknowable, hence this sign's reputation for the spooky, mysterious, or magical. Traditional astrology also tells us that the Moon and Scorpio make for a challenging combination. Taurus is the Moon's sign of "exaltation," her most fertile and comfortable place to be so, by definition, Scorpio is the Moon's sign of "fall," her most difficult placing.

Does this automatically translate into bad news? It can do, if we think of things like illness or death as "bad," and health and life as "good," but when we take a more holistic approach, we see that these Scorpio days are a crucial part of life's pattern, especially when it comes to deep healing. The ultimate Scorpio message is to attend not just to the visible body but to the invisible mind and spirit, too.

Scorpio correlates to the 8th House of the zodiac, which is where we locate the life-death-rebirth cycle, including life-saving surgery. Only surgeons see the otherwise invisible workings of our body. A textbook story comes from a client who was diagnosed with a brain aneurysm, an invisible ticking time bomb in her head. Her successful surgery and two recovery days in an intensive care unit were completed under a Scorpio Moon.

Scorpio-Moon days can often bring news of those who are ill, either seriously or sometimes terminally, prompting connections with our family and friends on a very deep, emotional level, or becoming actively involved in care. The Scorpio Moon intensifies coping with grief or recognizing the importance of the quality of life, and death. In the UK, the Terminally Ill Adults (End of Life) Bill passed its second reading in Parliament on November 29, 2024, when the Moon was in Scorpio. Although not ultimately passed into law, this bill would have legalized assisted dying for people who met certain criteria in England and Wales.

It follows then that one of the most positive ways of honoring this Moon is to connect with the spiritual world, in any way that is meaningful and magical for you. These days are rich for psychic moments. Work with crystals, get your tarot cards out, study your horoscope, book a psychic reading with a medium, or watch near-death experience videos. There's a great deal of both wonder and comfort in all of these things because it doesn't take long to be forcibly reminded that there's more to our life on planet Earth than meets the eye.

Feel Empowered

Scorpio rules all that is taboo, with sex at the beginning of the list and death at the end, so yes, there is a great deal of truth in the "sexy Scorpio" reputation. If you want to revitalize your sex life, then this Moon is on your side. However, if you're on the dating scene, or if you meet someone new under this Moon, then be aware of the power but also the dangers of sexual attraction. Unprotected sex is a no-no. Scorpio and Pluto both symbolize magnetism but are also linked to secrecy and affairs. Check out availability.

Love or hate, there are not many gray areas with Scorpio. Power issues can also loom large, often around money and hidden price tags, but bear in mind that all emotions are super intense when they arrive in this Moon's wrapper. Don't give in to despair. It's not unusual to experience a dark night of the soul—a period in one's life in which they feel terror, total despair, or that their life if over—especially as we travel toward the end of the sign, but Scorpio's essence is regeneration. This is seen most vividly in another symbol for this sign, the phoenix. This mythological bird's ability to withstand fire and rise from the ashes makes it a powerful image for the Scorpio hallmarks of resilience, endurance, and the ability to start over, completely from scratch if necessary.

It is one of life's truths that we don't know how strong we are until we have to be, and Moon in Scorpio days can often be some kind of testing ground that connects us with our resourcefulness. We're more likely to battle on with something difficult, challenging, or frustrating, determined not to be beaten. If you want to embark upon anything that's going to need resolve, willpower, and total focus then this Mars/Pluto sign is second to none.

How to Relax

The golden rule is to switch off and unplug, in every sense and especially in the evenings. There's an obsessive streak to this Moon that's a red flag for workaholism or any other kind of addictive lifestyle habits.

What to Wear

Mars always links us to red, but Scorpio/Pluto puts black at the top of the list, followed by purple. Go for whatever makes you feel sexy, and vamp it up for a night out.

When the Moon is in Sagittarius

Element: Fire

Mode: Mutable

Ruler: Jupiter

Symbol: The Archer

Broaden Your Horizons

The third sign of Gemini, ruled by the Winged Messenger Mercury, is all about language acquisition and early education, how we learn to communicate with others, and engage with our immediate surroundings. The opposite sign of Sagittarius and the 9th House of the zodiac encompass the same themes but with much broader brushstrokes. Here we locate higher education and wider horizons in every sense, how we navigate the world at large, for experience, understanding, and wisdom. Hence Sagittarius is known as the sign of "the higher mind."

The top keyword for Jupiter is expansion, whether it's stretching our minds and satisfying our thirst for knowledge, or discovering that there's so much more to the world than our own backyard. This freedom-loving Moon has a way of lifting our heads out of the demands of the here and now, and turning our gaze to the future. After the heaviness, fixity, or even claustrophobia of Scorpio, it's no wonder that we have itchy feet and feel the need to get away. When we find ourselves talking to family or friends about holidays, sun seeking, a long weekend, somewhere new, anywhere other than here, then we know that some major plans could be in the making.

So, fire those Archer's arrows and pursue them, wherever they may land. Jupiter just loves to sow seeds that will lead to success and abundance, so pay close attention to all ideas flitting through your mind, not just the ones relating to travel. Planning social events gets a big tick, and business moves made on these days should be notable by their entrepreneurial flavor. In terms of learning, Moon in Sagittarius days are heaven sent for studying, reading, and writing, everything from fiction to academia, for pleasure or with a view to getting published and reaching a large audience.

Whatever you're looking for, be prepared to go further afield than usual. The Sagittarius spirit loves things like shopping trips that involve a lot of different places, or ordering online from abroad.

With this Moon's eye on the future, also think ahead in other ways. The downside to this Moon is more haste, less speed—underestimating how long things take, how much free time you really have, and biting off more than you can chew. If you need to agree to any kind of deadline then build in as much flexibility as possible.

Conversely, if you're agreeing dates with other people, have it in mind that you could be dealing with those who are enthusiastic and eager to please you, but who haven't necessarily thought things through. Sagittarius is always full of the best intentions! On the subject of resolutions, these are not the best days for giving anything up. As a general rule, Sagittarius overdoes things but isn't suited to total abstinence either, so choose moderation over denial.

Break Routine and Follow Your Intuition

Back to daily life, try not to be chained to work or home. Don't worry about breaking your usual routine or rearranging your day at short notice if something appealing presents itself. This Moon is sporty and loves exercise, is adventurous, and favors being out and about. Note how you somehow run into the people you want to see or who can be of help to you, simply by finding yourself in the right place at the right time. This is often a lucky Moon and a generous one, too. Watch how you find the best deals, or how people suddenly start giving you things or picking up the bill, or vice versa.

Sagittarius exudes optimism and exuberance—positive qualities to tap into—but be tactful. You may notice people asking for your advice or opinions when what they really want is reassurance. Debates can get very heated, too, whether it's trouble at work, conflicting desires, or strident political or religious views.

Sagittarius also links to truth when dealing with matters of justice or litigation but, in or out of the courtroom, this Moon is when we're noticeably more concerned with being fair or doing what feels right. Honor your own ethical beliefs or back your intuition. These days are right for acting or deciding for reasons which reflect both our inner voice and our philosophy, regardless of what others might think.

How to Relax

This Fire sign finds it hard to hit the brake pedal and is especially prone to burnout. Slow down from a gallop to a saunter, and eat well rather than on the run. Switch off the world news.

What to Wear

Jupiter links to purples and the Sagittarian keywords are bright, bold, and free-flowing. Anything too small or too tight is a no-no for your look and comfort.

When the Moon is in Capricorn

Element: Earth

Mode: Cardinal

Ruler: Saturn

Symbol: The Mountain Goat

Focus on Your Goals

The fourth sign of Cancer rules everything to do with our home, family, and private life, while the opposite sign of Capricorn and the 10th House is where we locate our public life, including our ambitions, sense of purpose, and status out in the world. The previous sign of Sagittarius is about expansion, everything that makes our world bigger and better, and the reaction to this is contraction, the things that make our world smaller, if only temporarily.

As the Moon is "dignified" in the opposite sign of Cancer, she is therefore in "detriment" in this Saturn-ruled sign. Transferring those feminine lunar qualities of tending and nurturing to our working life is no easy feat, especially if you're a woman involved in a male-dominated, ruthless business culture. However, this Moon shows us what we want to achieve and what's needed to make that happen. In the process, we can learn a lot about the discipline of not allowing our minds to wander, minimizing distractions of all kinds, and simply getting the job done. This is a great Moon for "adulting," and working from home if you can ignore your phone and the countless domestic jobs that are always waiting for our attention. You'll know when you're avoiding your true purpose when you simply have to wash the kitchen floor.

Maintain a Can-Do Attitude

When the Moon is in Capricorn, it's time to get focused, sometimes to the extent of putting on blinkers and working on one concern to the exclusion of all else. The Mountain Goat looks where it's putting its feet but is otherwise intent on only one thing—reaching the summit. There's no need to look back or sideways. In this respect, we can see then that Capricorn isn't about rushing or watching what everyone else is doing. Feverish competitiveness tends to belong more to the Fire signs, while the Earth signs materialize their results, stage by definite stage. Capricorn loves serious time management and a project.

This Moon is a wonderful symbol for professional women, especially those who are already climbing a corporate ladder or who are self-employed. On these days, the influence of powerful role models and those in a position to help us can make a significant difference. Note how you'll also hear about the accomplishments and empire-building feats of relatives or the other important women in your life. This Moon can bring recognition in the shape of praise or certificates.

We start to get the message that it's not enough just to feel vaguely ambitious, and that there's no substitute for effort, whatever the desire. Approach all your own challenges with a "can-do" perseverance, drive a hard bargain, and strip things back to basics. Step into your own authority, especially when up against any kind of system or those trying to make your decisions for you. Ask for guarantees, fix definite dates and times, set your intentions, and identify your true goals. In this spirit, the Moon in Capricorn days can be highly productive, in the present moment but also in terms of creating those vital stepping stones toward your future life.

Be Kind to Yourself and Others

Emotionally, this isn't the best Moon for intimacy as we can experience others as uncaring or unemotional, or even cold and unforgiving. If anyone closes down on you then don't try to force their hand. Ride it out for a couple of days rather than risk making matters worse. With this Moon, others are more likely to act or decide for their own unexplained reasons, based on priorities or values that might be very different from our own.

Capricorn asks us to be respectful, rather than irritated. Similarly, remember that you don't have to risk your own vulnerability with those who tend to be judgmental or hopelessly stuck in their own ways. Be aware of where you, too, might be judging. Some thoughts or feelings will be better kept to yourself.

Moon in Capricorn days can be hard going in other ways, too, such as feeling the weight of family duties, too many other responsibilities, or not enough free time. Try to create some. Toughen up when it comes to keeping needy people at bay and saying no to unreasonable demands. Capricorn has a way of testing our boundaries or making us learn things the hard way. Resolve not to learn the same lesson twice.

How to Relax

Don't take yourself too seriously. There's a lot of clever humor at the heart of Capricorn. Seek out your real friends for wisdom and laughter.

What to Wear

Capricorn's color is gray, which definitely doesn't have to be dreary or unsexy. Choose the right shade for you to create sophisticated, classic elegance.

When the Moon is in Aquarius

Element: Air

Mode: Fixed

Rulers: Saturn & Uranus

Symbol: The Water Bearer

Focus on Community and Connection

The Moon in the sign of the Water Bearer correlates with the 11th House where we locate the wider circle of people that are part of our world. On a universal level, this is the collective, the whole planet, but on a personal level, Aquarius is our own community, encompassing all our friends, colleagues, and social groups.

The opposite sign of Leo rules our personal creativity, how we shine and take center stage, but Aquarius is connected with sharing our pleasures, ideas, or concerns with like-minded others. Aquarius-Moon days are when we're more aware of needing to find or be with our tribe; when we need the sustenance of interacting with those who are on the same wavelength.

This is not to say that Aquarius isn't about individuality—far from it. The big paradox with this sign is that, although the focus is on others and how we are all connected, it's known for brilliance, originality, and outright quirkiness, often being one step ahead of the crowd. Be aware of your own talents, of what makes you "different," and observe how others are drawn to you on these days, and you to them.

Stand Up for What You Believe In

Like Capricorn, the other Saturn sign, this is a mindful Moon but not because of any rule book, tradition, or because someone else says so. This Moon is when we step in because we see a situation or another person from our own unique perspective. When we know that something is ethically wrong or right, we can move from a position of great strength, so this Moon can show us how to act for our own reasons, ones that don't necessarily make sense to others, even those who know us well.

Aquarius-Moon days are not designed for conforming for the sake of it, or just to keep the peace. You don't have to be an out-and-out rebel but honor your own values, insights, and act quietly on the strength of personal convictions. Back any cause that's close to your heart.

The other paradox to watch out for, however, is that there are always two sides to a story or different ways of looking at things. We might need to take that message on board, or get that message across to someone else—it can work both ways. Also, even a so-called expert can get it wrong. Seek alternatives or second opinions, especially with anything medical or connected to your rights.

Network and Interact With Others

As with all the communicative Air signs, Aquarius-Moon days are generally busy in terms of notably more than the average amount of connection and interaction with other people. With Uranus being the technology whiz kid, this primarily shows in our online life, often with moments that remind us of the power of the internet.

Arguably the most positive Aquarian gifts are strength in numbers and the power of groups. When it comes to business, furthering your ambitions, and empire-building, these are the days to maximize and improve your use of social media. Networking could open up all kinds of new avenues. Bear in mind, too, the crucial importance of starting new ventures or projects at the right moment. For "going live," whether it's starting a WhatsApp group or launching a website, the closer you can get to that seminal 0 degrees of Aquarius, the better.

If you dream of better days and wanting to make your mark on the world, the red flag for these days is deadly time wasting of endless scrolling and filling your head with trivia. Set yourself limits and identify any other time bandits. Fresh starts are well starred under the scrutiny of objective Aquarius and these days are brilliant for getting organized, everything from making lists to appointments. Shamelessly exploit the loophole of not what you know but who you know while you're at it.

Last but definitely by no means least, this is the sign of friendship so put your social life high up on your list of priorities. There's still no substitute for meeting up in real life instead of on a screen. When it comes to invites, parties, holiday plans, just say yes.

How to Relax

Doing anything with your favorite friends. But we can also get "peopled out" with this Moon and there's nothing wrong in closing the doors and enjoying your own company.

What to Wear

With colors, go for metallics, like silver, or electric blues and greens. Style-wise, Aquarius follows no rules. Just choose the things that make your friends say, "that is so *you*!"

When the Moon is in Pisces

Element: Water

Mode: Mutable

Rulers: Jupiter & Neptune

Symbol: The Fishes

Be Aware of Heightened Emotions

The sign of the Fishes correlates to the 12th House of the zodiac where we locate a vast range of deeply personal experiences, from loss, grief, or sacrifice through to intense empathy and enlightenment. This is in stark contrast to the cooler climes of Aquarius, and it's little wonder that traditional astrology calls this House "the vale of tears." This doesn't mean that the Moon's monthly trip through this sign will inevitably bring suffering, but more often than not we do come up close and personal with the world of feelings or health, for good or ill.

Starting with tears or fears, these Neptunian days are when worries can inflate into hot-air balloons, carrying us into the realms of soaring imagination and fearing the worst. Secret anxieties have a way of growing arms and legs, but the big question is: are they real? When we talk about our own fears, or listen to others talking about theirs, we see either that we're grappling with things that haven't even happened, or we can restore perspective with any issues that are genuine.

Joyful feelings can also bubble up and bring moments of very deep connection, either with another person or with an inner certainty of being on the right path. We may find ourselves following a dream, a creative vision, our instincts, all in a way that is often difficult to put into words but it "feels" right. Conversely, if something feels wrong, then it usually is. Don't go there!

Impose Boundaries and Take Control

Arguably the biggest challenge with this Moon is not to get swept along in the waves of other people's emotions, or our own. Like the sea, Pisces has no boundaries so we have to impose our own. Spot the difference between the person who has only their own best interests at heart rather than yours, and distinguish the sob stories from genuine need. Easier said than done, sometimes, this Moon has a way of presenting us with people or situations that tap into our guilty streak. We've all got one.

So, it helps to know that the undertow of seduction or manipulation can be very powerful, whether that's done unconsciously or as deliberate gaslighting. If you find yourself being sucked in to someone's whirlpool of woes or demands then take a breather before rushing to the rescue. Press that pause button and sift the facts from the feelings before you start jumping through hoops.

Sensitivity in all its guises is a major hallmark of these Pisces-Moon days. Things that we would normally brush off fairly quickly can work their way deeply into our emotional layers. It pays to do a spot-check on where we might be overreacting or if we're feeling sorry for ourselves. Ask yourself whether you're reading from the "poor me" script. Are you swimming upstream or downstream? Pisces is the archetype of both the Rescuer and the Victim.

On a more practical level, although this last sign is linked to retreat, it's my experience that these Piscean days don't allow much time for hiding out or just "going with the flow." More noticeably, we realize where we need to take control of a matter. Be proactive wherever possible, acting on what is needed and anticipating the problems, rather than reactive, dealing with the problems only as they're happening. This can save you a lot of angst.

Enjoy Company and Prepare for Closure

Ultimately, Pisces is about fusion, so this can be a very romantic and mystical Moon. It's also a very sociable one—let's not forget that larger-than-life benefic Jupiter is in the mix, too, and parties thrown under a Pisces Moon are often hugely entertaining ones where the wine and conversation flow, where our boundaries can dissolve in a good way, and we escape from our cares. Always have a designated driver when Pisces is about.

As the Moon arrives at the very end of Pisces, the last degree of the sign being also the last degree of the whole zodiac, we can expect decisive moments or natural endings. Closure is often about life steering us in a new direction, for fuzzy pictures snapping back into sharp focus, even if it's only to see what we can't have. It's revelation—and redemption. Accept what you need to give up to make something else viable. Or healthy.

How to Relax

Go swimming or be near water, whether it's the sea, a river, or a lake. For escapism, music, the arts, movies, wine bars, or bistros all hit the Pisces spot, or dance as if no one can see you.

What to Wear

Think sea greens, blues, and aquamarine; anything shimmery and free-flowing, as well as glittery makeup, nails, adornments, and accessories.

Chapter Three

Lunations and Eclipses

The Sun and the Moon are inextricably linked in a perennial cycle, expressed through their monthly union (New Moon) and their monthly opposition (Full Moon). Every six months these pairings manifest as a Solar and Lunar Eclipse. This precise lunar activity leads us into the world of prediction and is invaluable for the art of fine timing, both for life events and the unfolding of our key relationships.

Lunations

The Sun and the Moon have what is called a dyadic relationship, dependent on and defined by each other, and this becomes immediately apparent when we venture into the world of Moon astrology. When we look for the definition of "lunation," we find that this word refers to the amount of time that elapses between two New Moons. The average length of the lunar cycle is 29 days, with some very slight variations. This monthly cycle has been with us since the dawn of time, beginning with a New Moon, culminating with a Full Moon two weeks later, and then waning over the following two weeks to the time of the next New Moon. So, the astronomy works like this:

- The cycle begins with a New Moon, when the Moon is between the Earth and the Sun. The side of the Moon that is facing toward the Earth is in darkness; we can't see it.
- The cycle culminates with a Full Moon, when the Earth is between the Sun and the Moon. The side of the Moon that is facing toward the Earth is fully illuminated.

For the sake of astrological vocabulary, we refer to the exact moment of either a New or a Full Moon as a lunation.

In traditional astrology, the Sun and the Moon are known as the Lights, or the Luminaries, the Sun being the light of the day and the Moon being the light of the night. They're further dignified with their ancient titles of Lord of the Day and Lady of the Night. Unlike all of the planets, the Lights are never retrograde. This phenomenon refers to the times when, from our point of perspective here on planet Earth, the planets appear to make regular backward loops. These journeys in reverse last different lengths of times according to the cycle of the planet in question. For example, Mercury with his one-year cycle is always retrograde for three weeks at a time, whereas Jupiter with his 12-year cycle is always retrograde for four months at a time.

This phenomenon does not apply to the Lights, who hold their own steady courses, the Sun moving at the rate of one degree a day and the Moon approximately 12 degrees a day. They are knowable, unchangeable, and invaluable in the world of predictive astrology as they're linked to fine timing. I often think of them as "cats' eyes," those little lights that pick out the road ahead, acting as what is known as astrological "testimony" to the bigger journey. In other words, although lunations can be "stand-alone" powerful omens, they more usually support and confirm other astrological activity in a horoscope.

The Timings of New and Full Moons

Throughout the year, there is one New and one Full Moon for each of the 12 signs. This can be very slightly variable, occasionally going out of sync for a month in the event of a Blue Moon, which is a second Full Moon in a single calendar month—the first one at the very beginning of a month, and the second at the very end of that same month. This means that some years will have 25 lunations in total instead of the usual 24.

We see an example of this for 2026, with a Full Moon falling on both May 1 and 31, as shown in the table.

Full Moons

January 3 at 13 Cancer
February 1 at 13 Leo
March 3 at 13 Virgo (Lunar Eclipse)
April 2 at 12 Libra
May 1 at 11 Scorpio
May 31 at 10 Sagittarius
June 29 at 8 Capricorn
July 29 at 6 Aquarius
August 28 at 5 Pisces (Lunar Eclipse)
September 26 at 4 Aries
October 26 at 2 Taurus
November 24 at 2 Gemini
December 24 at 2 Cancer

New Moons

January 18 at 28 Capricorn
February 17 at 28 Aquarius (Solar Eclipse)
March 19 at 28 Pisces
April 17 at 27 Aries
May 16 at 26 Taurus
June 15 at 24 Gemini
July 14 at 22 Cancer
August 12 at 20 Leo (Solar Eclipse)
September 11 at 18 Virgo
October 10 at 17 Libra
November 9 at 17 Scorpio
December 9 at 17 Sagittarius

We also immediately see that the New Moon is in the same sign as the Sun, and the Full Moon is in the opposite sign to the Sun. Never again will you have to ask yourself, what sign is the New or Full Moon? The Sun's journey is all we need to know. For example, if we're in the Capricorn time of year (from the Winter Solstice on December 21 through to January 20) then the New Moon has to fall in this sign, and the Full Moon has to fall in the opposite sign of Cancer.

These "at a glance" tables also illustrate how throughout the year we have a New and Full Moon for each sign, each pairing being in opposite signs, and that Eclipse season falls every six months. It is important to note that the themes of each sign, as explored in Chapter 2, are likely to be especially significant or intensified at the times of lunations.

Go to the Resources section on page 140 for information on how to look up all the lunations in a given year.

Universal vs Particular

All lunations and Eclipses are significant at a *universal* level—that is, we see them working out in the world around us. They're also important at a *particular* level, in terms of events in the lives of individuals, when they line up with natal planets or Angles. In other words, when working with any particular horoscope, do the lunations "match up" with the natal planets or with any of the four sensitive Angles—Ascendant/Descendant or M.C./I.C. (see pages 24–25)?

"Matching up" means that the sign and degree need to correspond with the position of the natal planets or the Angles. The closer the match, the more significant the corresponding event. The main aspects (relationship between the two, see page 21) to look for are:

- Conjunctions (positioned in the same sign)
- Oppositions (positioned in opposite signs, e.g. a lunation in Aries would be opposite planets or Angles in Libra)
- Squares (positioned three signs apart either side, e.g. a lunation in Aries would be square to planets or Angles in Capricorn/Cancer)

What is the Symbolism of a New Moon?

The beginning of the lunar cycle is exactly that—a beginning. Astronomically, it's the moment each month when the Sun and the Moon are at exactly the same place, so at the same degree of the same sign. This is why we can't physically see the New Moon, she's lost in the Sun's glare, so when we do see that wafer-thin crescent in the sky, the New Moon is, in fact, already two to three days old.

Astrology's job is always to convert the astronomical information into meaning. The New Moon is the "seed" moment for a new anything, ranging from external material matters to our internal world of personal development and progress—for example, the conception of babies or ideas, receiving new information that makes a difference, the arrival of new faces, finding a new job, or making fresh starts of any kind. As the Moon correlates to the 4th House of the horoscope—the sector that's the natural domain of the sign of Cancer (family, home, property)—the New Moon in any sign is especially significant for news concerning relatives, for any kind of house hunting, or for finding a buyer or a tenant.

We can also choose the time of the New Moon for conscious behavior, such as setting intentions or starting a project, but more usually we find that the "newness" relates to things coming into our lives simply because the time is right.

So, pay attention to anything or anyone who's playing a noticeable role in your life at these times, but bear in mind that the symbolism of the invisibility of the New Moon also needs to be observed. This means that we may not always be aware of the moment a seed is sown, but it becomes apparent in the days or even weeks that follow, exactly as with the conception of a child.

What is the Symbolism of a Full Moon?

Astronomically, the Full Moon is that moment each month when the Moon is exactly opposite the Sun, thus all of the orb of the Moon is receiving the Sun's light.

Symbolically, the Full Moon is lunacy, the monthly madness. Frontline workers and first responders in police stations, hospitals, or any kind of emergency unit will confirm this to be true. However, it's also about much more than the "domestics" and the emotional tides riding high. On the plus side, here is the fruition moment, when a matter comes full circle, ripens, and delivers results. The link to women and fertility is unmistakable—the 29-day cycle starting with the seed moment, the Moon appearing to change shape every night as her belly swells, eventually reaching the perfect roundness of full-term pregnancy.

The Moon rules all that is feminine, and it's not uncommon for women living together to sync in their menstruation. Lunar gardening is a practice used by some farmers, following the Moon's phases to determine when to plant (conceive) or harvest (birth) their crops.

As children, we discover that the Full Moon is for witches who ride on their broomsticks with their black cats, especially at Halloween. This is the festival of Samhain that is celebrated by 37 countries, when the veil between our earthly existence and the spirit world is said to be at its thinnest. Most of us can remember drawing pictures of crones, with their pointed hats and magic wands.

So, the Full Moon is undeniably the witchy time of the month, when our instincts are sharpened and we may have a deeper sense of magic or wonder. This links into arguably the most important theme of any Full Moon, which is to illuminate. Expect themes of visibility, such as events that coax us out of the shadows and onto center stage, or processing that which has previously been unknown to us. The Full Moon is nearly always a time of helpful information or completion, anything from bringing secrets or hidden issues out into the open to clarifying the things that have been puzzling or murky. Suddenly, a matter takes on a different shape, the path ahead is floodlit, and the answers become increasingly obvious.

Finding Relevant Lunations in Your Own Chart

Working with "retrodiction" (what's already shown) as opposed to "prediction" (what lies ahead) is arguably the best way to learn astrology. With new clients, I always start readings with some retrodiction so that I can demonstrate how their horoscope has worked in the past. Lunations are clear and often very powerful examples for this kind of exploration.

You will need your Ephemerides (see page 140)—the collection of tables that lists the planetary motion for every single day and which also shows the date, sign, and degree of New and Full Moons, and the dates for when these are Eclipses. Choose any big event in your life and you will nearly always find that it matches up with a lunation.

If you see two lunations in a row matching up with your own horoscope then this underlines the importance of that time period. If you see a series of three or more lunations in a row, the message is even stronger—a major life event will be unfolding during this time.

Timing

What time span does "matching up" cover? It is perfectly possible for a New/Full Moon or Eclipse to fall on the exact day of the corresponding life event, small or large, but more usually you can expect to see a timescale of a few days either side. Sometimes we see a timescale of up to two weeks either side of an event—that is, the time since the previous lunation and the time to go before the next one.

The 44th President of the United States Barack Obama's chart is an example of this as, along with the dominance of Jupiter activity, the rest of the supporting picture is all related to the Moon. This includes his Lunar Return (see Chapter 4) and lunations, a series of five in total, starting with the one that occurred nine days before his inauguration on January 20, 2009, and then the next four, all corresponding with his first two months in office.

- January 11: The lunation prior to the inauguration date was a Full Moon at 21 Cancer, opposite Obama's Saturn 25 Capricorn (His rising sign is Aquarius, making Saturn his chart ruler.)
- January 26: The following lunation was a New Moon/Solar Eclipse at 6 Aquarius, conjunct his Jupiter 0 Aquarius.
- February 9: Full Moon/Lunar Eclipse 21 Leo, conjunct his Descendant 18 Leo/ Uranus 25 Leo (His rising sign is Aquarius, making Uranus his co-ruler.)
- February 25: New Moon 6 Pisces, conjunct his Chiron 5 Pisces.
- March 11: Full Moon 21 Virgo, conjunct his Mars 22 Virgo.

Examples of the New Moon in Action

Celine Dion

Whenever we look at the astrology for the conception or birth of children, the Moon is, unsurprisingly, a crucial factor. After years of failed fertility treatments and one heartbreaking miscarriage, Celine Dion and husband René Angélil finally celebrated the birth of their first child René-Charles on January 25, 2001. The birth was within 15 hours of a New Moon that aligned with both Celine and René's horoscopes, picking up the stunning synastry between them as they share the same "me–you" horizon of the Ascendant–Descendant. For Celine, this is 2 Leo–2 Aquarius; for René, the horizon is 1 Leo–1 Aquarius.

René-Charles was born on January 25, 2001, and there was a New Moon on January 24, 2001. A New Moon falls in the same sign as the Sun, so this lunation was at 4 Aquarius. This fell conjunct (to within 5 degrees) of his parents' shared Descendants, the super sensitive Angle that marks the beginning of the 7th House of marriage and partnership.

Since René Angélil's death in January 2016, their Aquarian child has grown to take up the role of partner as well as son. These days, he's known to provide his mother with significant support, including assistance at her now rare public appearances, as she battles with her ongoing health issues.

Celine called René-Charles their "miracle baby" and used a frozen embryo from that same IVF process to conceive again, years later. Her twin sons, Nelson and Eddy, were born on October 23, 2010, within 12 hours of a Full Moon at 29 Aries, exactly conjunct Celine's natal Moon, also 29 Aries. This is an example of quite exquisite astrological timing that reminds us over and over that something bigger than us is always at work.

An IVF Baby

During the writing of this chapter, I did a reading for a new client, who I will call Ruth. With the synchronicity that so often happens with astrological work, it turned out that her story mirrored Celine Dion's. Again, there was a history of heartache with failed IVF treatments, but one last attempt in 2023, in her early 40s, bore fruit.

On May 19, 2023, there was a New Moon 28 Taurus, the Moon's sign of "exaltation" and her most fertile placing. This fell conjunct Ruth's Ascendant of 0 degrees Gemini to within 2 degrees. The Ascendant often shows at times of conception as this is the sensitive Angle that marks the beginning to the 1st House of the physical body.

On May 22, 2023, Ruth received her IVF treatment, on beautifully prepared astrological ground, and a healthy daughter was born the following January. Pure joy!

Prince Harry, Duke of Sussex

Born September 15, 1984, 16:20 BST, London

Many of my examples of astrology at work are taken from the horoscopes of the British royal family. This is because, regardless of whether we're interested in the monarchy or not, the lives of the individuals are an invaluable source of learning material. They all have accurate times of birth, so we know that we're working with precise horoscopes, and also their life events are in the public eye and crucial timelines are easily researched.

New Moons often feature at times of marriage, which is symbolically appropriate since starting a new life links into the Moon's domain of home, family, daily routines, and emotional needs. On May 15, 2018, we had a New Moon at 24 Taurus, and the wedding of Prince Harry and Meghan Markle took place on May 19, 2018.

The top synastry between the pair (matching points in their horoscopes, see page 29) is his Moon 21 Taurus conjunct her Chiron 22 Taurus. My own view is that the astrology shows us how Meghan was able to take up a healing role (Chiron) and meet Harry's needs (Moon) in terms of both his mental and physical health. The trauma of his mother Diana's tragedy would inevitably play a role in his marriage, and he famously quit the habits of cigarettes, alcohol, and caffeine while supporting Meghan through her first pregnancy.

Examples of the Full Moon in Action

Queen Elizabeth II

Born April 21, 1926, 02:40 BST, London

Queen Elizabeth II's first child was Charles, born November 14, 1948, 21:14 GMT, London. As we would expect, there was plenty of other symbolically accurate astrological activity to announce his arrival, but also a lunation to support the bigger picture and to zoom us in closer to the actual date. Within 48 hours of the birth, there was a Full Moon that aligned with the Queen's horoscope.

There was a Full Moon on November 16, 1948, two days after Charles's birth. A Full Moon falls in the opposite sign to the Sun, in this case Scorpio, so this lunation was 24 Taurus. This fell exactly conjunct the Queen's I.C. of 25 Taurus. One of the super sensitive four Angles (see page 24), the I.C. is the beginning to the 4th House of home, roots, and origins, and is where we would locate the continuation of the family line.

King Charles III

In terms of bringing things to light, a Full Moon can be an important moment for revealing health matters, too. On January 25, 2024, the Full Moon was at 5 Leo, exactly conjunct Charles's Ascendant (beginning of the 1st House of the physical body), also 5 Leo. On the day, the Full Moon fell opposite Pluto at 0 Aquarius—both 0 (beginnings) and 29 (endings) are known as the "critical degrees" (see page 71). Charles has a Sun in Scorpio, with his natal Pluto (Scorpio's planet) in his 1st House.

On January 26, 2024, Charles underwent a corrective procedure for a benign enlarged prostate, less than 18 hours after the Full Moon. On February 5, 2024, it was announced that the corrective surgery had revealed cancer, the type not named other than to say it wasn't prostate. A long period of treatment lay ahead.

Vivien Leigh

A Full Moon can be a supportive factor in stories of success or even the beginning of fame. When actress Vivien Leigh visited the "Burning of Atlanta" set of *Gone with the Wind*, director David O. Selznick famously saw her face lit up in the flames. What a stunning evocation of Full Moon symbolism. Having spent two years auditioning more than 1,400 hopefuls, he knew instantly that his long search for the perfect Scarlett O'Hara was over.

- Vivien visited the set on December 10, 1938, and on December 7 there was a Full Moon 14 Gemini, which fell conjunct her career planet Saturn 17 Gemini.
- On January 13, 1939, her casting as Scarlett O'Hara was announced, and on January 5 there was a Full Moon 14 Cancer, opposite her Jupiter 13 Capricorn (the opportunity planet, powerful in the 9th House, Jupiter's domain, ruling all that is international).
- *Gone with the Wind* was released on December 15, 1939, and on December 10 there was a New Moon 18 Sagittarius, opposite her Saturn 17 Gemini.

Until this role, Vivien Leigh was a minor British actor, but her portrayal of the willful and complex Scarlett shot her to international stardom.

We find further confirmation of the Moon's vital role in what is called "the cosmic marriage" (see page 29), when one person's Sun matches the other person's Moon—Vivien Leigh (Moon 9 Aquarius) and Clark Gable (Sun 12 Aquarius) costarred as Scarlett O'Hara and Rhett Butler.

Eclipses

Every six months we enter Eclipse season, and these always work in pairs—a Solar Eclipse on a New Moon followed by a Lunar Eclipse on a Full Moon, or vice versa. Very occasionally we see three Eclipses in a row, two Solar Eclipses with the Lunar one in the middle, or two Lunar Eclipses with the Solar one in the middle.

At the time of writing, the most recent examples of these were in 2018 and 2020:

- 2018: July 13 New Moon and Solar Eclipse at 20 Cancer; July 27 Full Moon and Lunar Eclipse at 4 Aquarius; August 11 New Moon and Solar Eclipse at 18 Leo.
- 2020: June 5 Full Moon and Lunar Eclipse at 15 Sagittarius; June 21 New Moon and Solar Eclipse at 0 Cancer; July 5 Full Moon and Lunar Eclipse at 13 Capricorn.

The next time we'll see three in a row will be in 2027: July 18 Full Moon and Lunar Eclipse at 25 Capricorn; August 2 New Moon and Solar Eclipse at 10 Leo; August 17 Full Moon and Lunar Eclipse at 24 Aquarius.

Lunations are an integral part of the timeline of an unfolding event, but when they happen to be Eclipses, too, then we're looking at tipping points. In other words, Eclipses are like supercharged lunations and carry some kind of finality, reflecting the events and changes that tell us that life will never be the same again, as we'll see in the coming examples.

The most important starting point when it comes to understanding Eclipses is to observe the celestial logistics. It is only because the Sun and the Moon appear to us to be the same size in our skies that the wonder of Eclipses can happen at all, the disk of one fitting exactly over the disk of the other.

This is the best illustration of the dyadic relationship between the Lights, which in turn reminds us that their apparent equal size gives them equal symbolic weight in the horoscope. Astrology, and particularly horoscopy, is never just about the Sun sign.

How Are Eclipses Created?

Eclipses occur every six months when a New or Full Moon is also conjunct the Moon's North and South Nodes, the imaginary points at which the Moon cuts across the Ecliptic (from which we derive the word "Eclipse"), which is the apparent path of the Sun's motion as seen from planet Earth. It's because the Earth's axis is tilted that we don't get Eclipses every month.

Back to symbolism, in traditional astrology, the line of the Moon's Nodes (always exactly opposite each other) symbolizes a dragon. The Sun and the Moon (the Lights) are the eyes of the dragon, and the dragon "eating" the Lights refers to the phenomenon of eclipses:

- The North Node (*Caput Draconis*) is depicted as the head of the dragon and is regarded as fortunate, as this is where the dragon feeds and gains nourishment. This can include good karma.
- The South Node (*Cauda Draconis*) is depicted as the tail of the dragon and is regarded as unfortunate, being where the dragon excretes. This can include bad karma.

Since Eclipses work in pairs (very occasionally in threes), a Lunar Eclipse (on a Full Moon) is therefore always followed two weeks later by a Solar Eclipse (on a New Moon) or vice versa.

- A Lunar Eclipse occurs when the Moon is obscured by the shadow of the Earth at the time of a Full Moon.
- A Solar Eclipse occurs when the Sun is obscured by the shadow of the Moon at the time of a New Moon.

Eclipse Symbolism

Eclipses get mixed press but, essentially, they're points of significant change that often involve power issues and/or the crux points of triangular situations, i.e. as symbolized by the intricate relationship between the three bodies of the Sun, the Moon, and the Earth. Who is going to overshadow whom?

There is often a flavor of death/rebirth symbolism—changing colors, the light disappearing and coming back on again, establishing a new order. These times are generally not easy but, when the shadows lift, a new landscape is revealed and we find ourselves being moved on.

There's a lot of conflicting information out there about how long Eclipses are operative for. Some say weeks or even longer, but over the years of observation I've come to find that their duration is usually much shorter. Yes, effects are long-lasting and often life-changing, but the actual events that clearly match Eclipse symbolism often fall either on or very close to the actual date.

Examples of Eclipses in Action

Edward VIII—The Most Famous Royal Abdication

A clear and powerful example of a Solar Eclipse at work is the abdication of Edward VIII, for the sake of a woman, Wallis Simpson. The Eclipse symbolism in the horoscope of his younger brother, George VI, who had kingship thrust upon him, is unmistakable.

On December 10, 1936, Edward VIII officially abdicated and on December 13, a Solar Eclipse fell at 22 Sagittarius. His brother George VI was born on December 14, 1895, placing his Natal Sun at 22 Sagittarius, so exactly conjunct the Eclipse degree.

The Sun (who incidentally rules kingship at a universal level) in George's natal chart is conjunct the 3rd House cusp—the sensitive beginning of the House of siblings. His brother is eclipsed, and George is crowned in Edward's place. The pairing Lunar Eclipse two weeks later on December 28, 1936 fell at 6 Cancer, conjunct Edward's Sun 2 Cancer (sign of home and family), and Edward spent the rest of his life in the shadows of exile.

Death of George VI—Elizabeth II Becomes Queen

In her early years, Elizabeth was considered a minor royal, but destiny had other ideas. Her life changed dramatically with Edward VIII's abdication, because her father, George VI, then became King, making her the heir presumptive (assuming no boys were subsequently born) at the tender age of 10.

With the early death of George VI aged just 56, Elizabeth became Queen much earlier than was generally expected—on the day, February 6, 1952, she was only 25 years old. On February 11, there was a Lunar Eclipse at 21 Leo, and on February 25, there was a Solar Eclipse at 5 Pisces.

With her Sun in Taurus, Elizabeth II had her Moon in Leo but early on in the sign, 12 degrees. It was her Neptune at 22 Leo that picked up the Lunar Eclipse. The shadow of the death of her father automatically elevated her to the role of monarch, a role she was destined to play for the next 70 years. This is textbook Eclipse symbolism.

What about her husband? Life changed suddenly for Prince Philip, too, as shown by the Solar Eclipse at 5 Pisces falling conjunct his natal Uranus (the unexpected, the rug puller) at 9 Pisces, posited in his 7th House of marriage. Life for both of them would never be the same again.

Prince William and Prince Harry—Brotherly Conflict

In December 2019 through January 2020, we had history repeating itself with the tale of two brothers, Prince William accepting the mantle of responsibility and Prince Harry stepping back from his royal life for the sake of his wife. These events were also reflected in Eclipse symbolism—on December 26, 2019, there was a Solar Eclipse at 4 Capricorn; two weeks later, on January 10, 2020, there was a Lunar Eclipse at 20 Cancer.

The Solar (masculine) Eclipse picked up natal positions for William and Harry, followed by the Lunar (feminine) Eclipse picking up natal positions for their wives, Kate and Meghan. The Solar Eclipse at 4 Capricorn was conjunct Harry's natal Jupiter at 3 Capricorn and opposite William's Sun at 0 Cancer and Moon at nearly 5 Cancer; the Lunar Eclipse at 20 Cancer was conjunct Meghan's Ascendant at 24 Cancer and opposite Kate's Sun at 19 Capricorn and conjunct her Moon at 21 Cancer.

There was no going back—a shadow fell over the relationship between the two brothers who began living separate lives in different countries.

William and Kate, Prince and Princess of Wales

Those who are born on Eclipses are often very sensitive to all lunations, and especially other Eclipses. The Moon astrology between William and Kate borders on the spooky and definitely has the feel of destiny.

We have Eclipses every six months, and the pair were born six months apart in Eclipse seasons.

- William's natal Lights are Moon 5 Cancer and Sun 0 Cancer. He was born on the Equinox June 21, 1982, the same day as a New Moon (Sun and Moon together in the same sign), which was also a Solar Eclipse.
- Kate's natal Lights are Moon 18 Cancer and Sun 19 Capricorn. She was born on January 9, 1982, the same day as a Full Moon (Sun and Moon opposite each other), which was also a Lunar Eclipse.

The most powerful showing of Eclipse symbolism for them after Harry's departure came in the spring of 2024. Remember that the most important aspects from natal planets to the degree of any lunation or Eclipse are conjunctions (same sign), oppositions (opposite sign), or squares (three signs apart, either side). There is also a school of thought that says Solar Eclipses are about men and Lunar Eclipses are about women, and there's a perfect illustration of that above with the two couples, but this is by no means an invariable rule. It was the Solar Eclipse that revealed Kate's health crisis.

On March 22, 2024, Kate released a personal video announcing that her abdominal surgery had revealed cancer and that she would be starting preventative chemotherapy. On March 25, there was a Lunar Eclipse at 5 Libra and on April 8, there was a Solar Eclipse at 19 Aries.

The Solar Eclipse was exactly conjunct Chiron who was also at 19 Aries on the day. Chiron is known as the Wounded Healer and is often prominent at times of illness and recovery. The Solar Eclipse fell in an exact square to Kate's natal Eclipse, the Sun at 19 Capricorn/Moon at 18 Cancer, who in turn are both square to her Saturn 21 Libra (opposite sign to Aries). Also note that her Full Moon is "cuspal"—falling across the beginning (extra sensitive/magnified) of the 6th/12th Houses of health (6th) and treatment/confinement (12th).

In her public role, we see Kate's Capricorn side, the epitome of a confident businesswoman who married into "The Firm," the Mountain Goat who never puts a foot wrong. When her illness was diagnosed, we saw the personal side, the self-protective Moon in Cancer who announced calmly but firmly that she would be focusing on healing, and immediately retreated into the private shell of her home to do so. The importance of obvious family themes (Moon/Cancer) rang out loud and clear as she made it apparent that she and Prince William would be managing the situation privately, primarily for the sake of their young children.

Nicole Kidman and Keith Urban—Relationship Breakup

It was shocking breaking news when it was announced on September 29, 2025, that Nicole Kidman and Keith Urban had been living apart for several months and had separated after 20 years together. Nicole filed for divorce the following day, citing irreconcilable differences. To the outside world, this had been a solid marriage.

As to be expected, there was very strong and clear symbolically accurate astrology happening in both horoscopes and there were Eclipses at work when the breakup hit the headlines.

On September 7, 2025, there was a Lunar Eclipse at 15 Pisces—this was square Nicole's Moon at 13 Sagittarius, and opposite Keith's Venus at 15 Virgo. On September 21, there was a Solar Eclipse at 29 Virgo—this was square Nicole's Sun at 29 Gemini and opposite her Chiron at 29 Pisces, and it was conjunct Keith's Uranus at 27 Virgo and opposite his Chiron at 26 Pisces.

It was reported that Nicole did not want the divorce, hence waiting until the last minute to file, but relationships that come unstuck under Eclipses are done and dusted. This can be shown just by the Eclipse but more usually the Eclipse lies at the heart of other unfolding astrology, and often acts as the final moment of truth. Lunar activity is the fine timing and decisive factor in the mix.

Affairs are nearly always the cause of Eclipse breakups. The shadow falls, in the shape of a third party, and the triangular dance between the three bodies of the Sun, the Moon, and the Earth comes into play. Note how both of the September 2025 Eclipses picked up Nicole's Lights. Double trouble. Also, the wounding of Chiron is present for both.

With the Lunar Eclipse falling exactly opposite Keith's Venus (a woman, love) and then the Solar Eclipse falling on his Uranus (shocks, surprises, the divorce planet), the most likely interpretation for the split was a new love, but rumors have never been substantiated and the details, for now, remain private.

The Love Triangle of Brad Pitt, Jennifer Aniston, and Angelina Jolie

Arguably one of the best-known love triangles of all started in the summer of 2004 when Brad Pitt and Angelina Jolie met on the set of the movie *Mr and Mrs Smith*, while he was married to Jennifer Aniston.

On January 7, 2005, Jennifer and Brad's separation was publicly announced, and she filed for divorce two months later. On October 2, the divorce was finalized, at the point when Angelina would have been about one month into her first pregnancy. The very next day, on October 3, a Solar Eclipse at 10 Libra picked up their key three-way synastry, falling exactly opposite Jennifer's natal Venus at 9 Aries, Brad's natal Jupiter at 9 Aries, and Angelina's natal Mars at 10 Aries. Two weeks later, on October 17, the pairing Lunar Eclipse at 24 Aries fell exactly conjunct Jennifer's Descendant (marriage Angle) 24 Aries and Angelina's natal Chiron at 26 Aries.

Even though the Jolie-Pitt relationship broke up 12 years later, it was the Eclipse symbolism that told the story at the time, and which made the point that Brad's marriage to Jennifer Aniston was totally irretrievable.

Matthew Perry

The hugely popular actor Matthew Perry (August 19, 1969–October 28, 2023) was open about his life of struggle with alcohol and drug addiction. It's also well-documented that the six members of *Friends* were very close and that his five costars all supported him as much as they possibly could, but ultimately to no avail.

Matthew Perry died on October 28, 2023, exactly on the second of the two Eclipses in that month—Solar Eclipse at 21 Libra on October 14 and Lunar Eclipse at 5 Taurus on October 28. The Lunar Eclipse picked up his natal Moon at 7 Scorpio, involved in the toughest aspect (the relationship of one planet to another) in his horoscope. In addition to being in a difficult sign, as Scorpio is the Moon's sign of "fall," we see that his Moon at 7 Scorpio sits opposite Saturn at 9 Taurus. Any natal combinations of the Lights with Saturn are challenging and often speak of a difficult start in life.

In traditional astrology, Saturn is known as "the enemy of the Lights," as the Sun and Moon are the life forces, whereas Saturn is ultimately the Grim Reaper. This is reflected in the fact that the Lights are strong in the signs where Saturn is weak, and vice versa, as shown in the table—for example, Saturn is in detriment in Cancer, which is the Moon's sign of dignity; Saturn is exalted in Libra, which is the Sun's sign of fall (see pages 16–17).

Planet	Dignity	Exaltation	Detriment	Fall
Sun	Leo	Aries	Aquarius	Libra
Moon	Cancer	Taurus	Capricorn	Scorpio
Saturn	Aquarius Capricorn	Libra	Leo Cancer	Aries

With the Moon as emotional needs sitting opposite Saturn, who can block or deny, the early damage can be extreme. In spite of endless attempts at rehab and therapy, Matthew was never able to heal from the neglect and lovelessness that arose from his parents' separation when he was just a baby. He was only 14 when his problems with alcohol began.

When dramatic events take place, good or bad, these can be seen in the horoscopes of those closest to the individual. For Courteney Cox, it was her second Saturn Return. (A Return is when a planet returns to the degree and sign as seen in our natal horoscope—for Saturn, the first return is in our 29th year, and the second is when we are 58/59 years old.) A Saturn Return is a time that is formative in many ways but often linked to a bereavement.

For the other four Friends, the tragedy showed through the Eclipses. The worst showing of being eclipsed is to be plunged into darkness. A very large light went out.

- The Solar Eclipse at 21 Libra on October 14, 2023, was opposite Jennifer Aniston's Saturn 21 Aries (conjunct her Descendant 24 Aries) and opposite Lisa Kudrow's Jupiter 19 Aries. Lisa was especially close to Matthew—they shared the same Sun and Moon signs, and his Venus 18 Cancer exactly matches her Ascendant of 18 Cancer.
- The Lunar Eclipse at 5 Taurus on October 28, 2023, was opposite Matt LeBlanc's Mars 2 Scorpio and opposite David Schwimmer's Sun/Venus conjunction at 8/9 Scorpio.

Jennifer Aniston spoke for all of the Friends when, in spite of the grief, she expressed a sense of relief that Matthew Perry was "out of pain." The Matthew Perry Foundation was created five days after his death, to provide treatment and reduce stigma for those in recovery, honoring his wish that he be remembered for helping others rather than just for the role of Chandler Bing. This is a top example of how the lifting shadows of an Eclipse reveal the imagery of death and rebirth, in this case leaving a lifesaving legacy for now and for generations to come.

Your Eclipse Checklist—What to Expect

Here are some key themes to look out for during each Eclipse season, which I have compiled over years of close observations.

- Being overshadowed or feeling in the dark.
- Themes of empowerment or disempowerment.
- Transferal of power, such as abdication, or any handing over of the reins.
- Themes of finality or inevitability—Eclipses light a fuse that can't be extinguished.
- Themes of loss/endings that change your life and set you on a different path.
- Themes of symbolic death/rebirth—out with the old, in with the new, literally or psychologically.
- Sorting winners from losers between twos or threes (Sun, Moon, Earth), e.g. affairs, job applications or promotions, house buying, any competitive or triangular situation. One person's loss is another person's gain.
- Dealing with that which, until the Eclipse, had been hidden from us in some way.
- Revelations—sometimes on the run up to the Eclipse, sometimes even exactly on the day.
- Revelations in the future, near or far, whose origins can be traced back to the time of the Eclipse. We learn what happened when we weren't looking, when we were in the dark, or "when the light went out."
- Tipping points of change or goodbyes—no going back to something belonging to your old life.

Locate in your own chart where an Eclipse will fall. The House(s) involved can give you clues (see pages 22–23)—remember that the Moon rules Cancer/4th House of home, family, property, so all related issues are extra sensitized during Eclipse seasons. Also remember that, in terms of astrological symmetry, the themes of the Houses work in pairs of opposites.

Chapter Four

Taking Moon Astrology Further

There are a variety of astrological "timing measures"—techniques that show how the planets move on after the moment of birth, and align with the natal chart to reflect life events. For the fast moving Moon, the most important of these are the progressed Moon, and the additional horoscope cast for the moment that the Moon returns to her natal position every four weeks.

The Progressed Chart

Your natal chart is the map of the planets as seen from Earth at the time and place of birth. This works at two levels—as your frozen moment in time that captures everything about you, but also as your own piece of celestial machinery that starts churning from the moment you are born. Predictive astrology therefore approaches the horoscope as a mechanism in perpetual motion. The wheels never stop turning.

What are the "timing measures" in astrology when it comes to prediction? There are many different techniques out there but in traditional astrology, these are the big three:

- A transit: A planet in the heavens arriving at the same degree as a natal planet or Angle.
- A progression: An alignment being formed between two planets, or between a planet and an Angle, in the progressed chart.
- The Moon: Either a New or Full Moon, including Eclipses, or the Progressed Moon aligning with a natal planet or Angle.

The major milestones on our journey, such as relationships, children, and career moves, are always shown either by a transit or a progression, or both. These in turn are then nearly always supported by a lunation or the position of the progressed Moon, so usually we're looking at a combination of these three different factors.

If you look back (retrodiction) at the astrology for the major events in your own life, you will find at least two of these features working together, if not all three. If you see two or all three of these features coming together in the future (prediction) then you can expect a major life event at that time. Astrological activity, showing us how things are moving on, always correlates to life events on planet Earth.

What are Transits? (Literal, In Real Time)

To locate transits, you will need Ephemerides, daily tables which list the motion of the planets, and the date and positions of the New/Full Moons and Eclipses (see page 111). On any given date, you then compare the position of the planets on that day to the planets in the horoscope, noting the alignments (called aspects, see page 21) being formed from the transiting (moving) planets to the natal (stationary) planets.

In terms of transits, the slower-moving planets are the most important—Jupiter, Saturn, Uranus, Neptune, Pluto, and Chiron. It's beyond the scope of this book to illustrate this enormous subject but it's covered in depth in another of my books, *Essential Astrology* (see page 141).

What are Progressions? (Symbolic)

The progressed chart works on the basis that each day subsequent to the date of birth corresponds to each year of the native's life. So, for example, the 30th day after the date of birth would correlate to the native's 30th year of life. The position of the planets on the 30th day shows the position of the progressed planets, that is, how far they have moved on by progression. The fully progressed chart also shows how the Angles have moved on.

On any given date, you then compare the position of the progressed planets to the planets in the natal horoscope, noting the aspects being formed from the progressed planets to the natal planets (called progressed to natal), or the aspects being formed from one progressed planet to another (called progressed to progressed).

In terms of progressions, the swifter-moving planets are the most important—the Sun, Mercury, Venus, and Mars. The Moon plays a unique role in the progressed chart because of her speed, as covered separately on page 28.

As progressions are a symbolic timing measure, we can't just look them up in the Ephemerides. They have to be calculated, and the astrologers who know how to do this by hand are a dying breed. Software has taken over which, of course, saves us hours of work but at the same time makes the process deceptively simple. Don't be fooled! Progressions are mathematically complex and must be used with absolute precision. In terms of our life story, they're crucially important because, like transits from the slower-moving outer planets, they can't be repeated in one lifetime. They're one-offs.

The Progressed Moon

To put the Moon's swiftness in perspective, let's start by noting that the Sun moves one degree a day, so in the progressed chart that converts to one degree a year. This means then that, by progression, the Sun moves at the rate of one sign every 30 years.

The Moon travels through the 12 signs approximately every 29 days, so in the progressed chart, that converts to 29 years. This means that, by progression, the Moon moves at the rate of one sign approximately every 2½ years. In this sense, the Moon is unique simply because it is not physically possible for any other planet to make the full orbit by progression in a lifetime.

Just like lunations, the position of the progressed Moon often acts as what is called a "testimony" to the bigger picture, confirming an event through appropriate symbolism and fine timing. As the Moon progresses around the whole chart, we can note lists of aspects but it's especially important to find when the progressed Moon is conjunct (same place) the natal planets or Angles, and also when she changes sign (approximately every 2½ years). If you want to do very detailed work, you can also use the other aspects (see page 21).

Examples of the Progressed Moon in Action

William and Kate, Prince and Princess of Wales

Life Event: Marriage, April 29, 2011

William's chart is an excellent working example at a natal and predictive level. He was born on a New Moon/Solar Eclipse (Sun 00.07 Cancer, Moon 04.57 Cancer) which is posited in his 7th House of partnership. This indicates a strong marriage.

- Progression: On the wedding day, progressed Venus (love, women) had literally just changed sign, reaching 00.01 Cancer and was therefore conjunct the natal Sun at 00.07 Cancer. 0 degrees, natal or progressed, is highly sensitized.
- Transit: The transit was Saturn—William was in the middle of his Saturn Return (once every 29 years, the first one known as the astrological coming of age), which lasted from mid-December 2010 to the beginning of September 2011. And, of course, he married a Saturn-ruled Capricorn.
- Lunation: To support this picture and to add to the finer timing, the progressed Moon on the wedding day was at 26 Cancer conjunct the progressed Sun at 27 Cancer. So, we see a progressed New Moon reflecting the natal one.

Kate was born on a Full Moon/Lunar Eclipse (Sun 19.12 Capricorn, Moon 18.41 Cancer). On the wedding day, Kate's progressed Moon was at 18.32 Leo opposite her progressed Sun at 19.11 Aquarius. So, we see a progressed Full Moon reflecting the natal one.

Meghan, Duchess of Sussex

Born August 4, 1981, 04:46 Canoga Park CA, USA
Life Event: Birth of first child, May 6, 2019

We locate children in the 5th House of the horoscope. In Meghan's chart we see the sign of Scorpio on the cusp of the 5th House so the significator for children is Mars (traditional ruler of Scorpio) or Pluto (co-ruler of Scorpio). On the day that her son Archie was born, we find:

- Progressed Mars 5.48 Leo sextile Saturn 5.52 Libra
- Progressed Mercury 12.00 Libra exactly sextile Sun 12.00 Leo
- Progressed Moon 11.46 Aquarius opposite Sun 12.00 Leo

Any planet progressed to the Sun (the life force) is an indication of a major life event and is especially apposite for the birth of a healthy child. Meghan is a Sun-ruled Leo with a Cancer Ascendant, so the Moon is her chart ruler. With the progressed Moon in Aquarius (opposite sign to Leo), the birth coincided with a progressed Full Moon (culmination), that happens only once every 29 years.

Catherine Zeta-Jones

Born September 25, 1969, 14:40 BST, Swansea, UK
Life Event: Proposal of marriage, December 31, 1999

Catherine Zeta-Jones and husband Michael Douglas famously share the same birthday, 25 years apart. Both romantic Librans! Michael Douglas proposed to her on the eve of a New Year and also of a new century.

We locate marriage partners in the 7th House of the horoscope. In Catherine's chart, we see:

- Sagittarius rising (the Ascendant), making the chart ruler Jupiter (ruler of Sagittarius).
- We therefore have the opposite sign of Gemini on the cusp of the 7th House (the Descendant), making the significator for her spouse Mercury (ruler of Gemini).
- In her natal chart, we find these two planets just three degrees apart—Mercury 10.13 Libra, Jupiter 13.19 Libra. Both are in the 9th House, where we locate foreigners and all matters overseas. Rulers of the 1st and 7th House sitting together is a textbook indication of a strong marriage.

On the day of the proposal, we find the love planet (Venus 02.58 Virgo in her natal chart) has joined her Mercury—progressed Venus 10.14 Libra conjunct her Mercury 10.13 Libra.

This works at a particular and a universal level (see page 112). Mercury is Catherine's partnership planet and also rules everything to do with the written and spoken word. What perfect astrology for the marriage (Venus) proposal (Mercury) that would change her life. The progressed Moon supports the timing, joining up with serious Saturn, planet of commitment and security, and also an indication of an older partner—progressed Moon 07.58 Taurus conjunct Saturn 07.53 Taurus.

Lunar Returns

Let's start by remembering that our birthday is our "Solar Return"—the day that the Sun has come full circle, returning to the degree and sign as seen in our natal horoscope. Hence we say "Many Happy Returns," wishing someone on their birthday many more years.

There is also something called the Solar Return chart, the horoscope cast for the moment that the Sun returns to the exact degree and minute that it holds in the natal horoscope. This is not a substitute for the natal chart but an extra chart, one specifically for your year ahead.

In keeping with this principle, there is also a chart for each of the Lunar Returns, which we might think means 12 a year, but that's a trick question. The Moon's cycle averages 29 days so we actually get 13 Lunar Returns in a year. Each one yields a horoscope in its own right for your month ahead, or "flavor of the month."

When I first started studying astrology over 40 years ago, we had to calculate all charts by hand, and the Lunar and Solar Returns were the most complex of them all. Precision is crucial in terms of arriving at the correct moment. Happily, being armed with pen, paper, a calculator, and a table of logarithms is now another world. These days we have the joy of astrological software, so all charts can be calculated with the press of a button.

Relocation

Most people do not live in their place of birth. However, there is no need to change the coordinates, even if someone has emigrated. For example, even though I've lived in Greece for over 30 years, I've found that my Solar and Lunar Return charts clearly work with my UK place of birth coordinates.

Interpreting Your Lunar Return

Approach your Lunar Return charts in the same way that you would start with a natal horoscope. It's beyond the scope of this book to cover the extensive art of chart interpretation but the same rules of craft apply. Here is a checklist as a guideline into locating meaning. You don't have to understand the whole chart, just zoom in on what is showing as important. (See Astrology Basics on pages 10–25 for information and visuals of the signs/planets, aspects, House meanings, and Angles.)

1. Locate the Moon and the Sun: The Moon, of course, will always be at exactly the same degree and minute as your natal Moon, it's just the House position that will change with every new chart. The Houses in which the Lights fall will give you a clue as to the most important themes of the month (see page 23).
2. Locate the chart ruler (and co-ruler if applicable): Which planet(s) rules the sign on the Ascendant? Assess its condition by sign/House/aspects.
3. Locate the ruler of the 7th House (and co-ruler if applicable): Which planet(s) rules the sign on the Descendant? This will be the primary significator for the partner or any significant other personally or professionally. Assess its condition by sign/House/aspects.
4. Look at the Angles: If a planet is conjunct one of the four sensitive Angles to within 5 degrees *either side*, then this planet is said to be "angular." This will turn out to be a dominant feature of the chart and therefore highly likely to carry the message of the month.
5. The inner House cusps: If a planet is conjunct one of the inner House cusps to within 2 degrees either side then this planet is also inviting extra attention, but to a lesser degree than planets on Angles.

Examples of Lunar Returns in Action

Queen Elizabeth II

Born April 21, 1926, 02:40 BST, London, UK
Life Event: Birth of first child Charles, November 14, 1948, London, 21:14 GMT

We saw in Chapter 3 how the birth of Charles was heralded by a Full Moon (see page 118), but does it also show in the Lunar Return for the relevant month? Yes, loud and clear, as we see the Lights picking out the Angles.

- Queen Elizabeth's Lunar Return that includes the date of the birth of her first child started on October 26, 1948. The Moon returned to her natal position at 07.53 GMT, so the Lunar Return horoscope is cast for that moment.
- In the Lunar Return chart, we find the Sun at 02.46 Scorpio, conjunct the Ascendant at 03.32 Scorpio.
- Her Moon 12.07 Leo is up on the Midheaven of 15.18 Leo.
- The co-ruler of Scorpio is Pluto, at 16.27 Leo in the chart, so also conjunct the Moon/Midheaven.
- At a personal level, the Ascendant is the beginning of the 1st House of the physical body and often shows at times of pregnancy/birth.
- At a universal level (see page 112), the Sun and Leo between them rule the monarchy and especially kingship.
- The event also shows clearly in her progressed chart as we see progressed Mercury (ruler of her 5th House of children) exactly conjunct her natal Sun at 0 Taurus. So, the Lunar Return confirms and amplifies the solar symbolism.

Barack Obama

Born August 4, 1961, 19:24 UT, Honolulu, USA
Life Event: Inauguration as President of the United States, January 20, 2009

It comes as no surprise to find that Jupiter, planet of opportunity, success, and freedom, played the lead role when Barack Obama was sworn in as the 44th President of the United States. Jupiter has an approximately 12-year cycle and Obama, then aged 47, was within two weeks of his fourth Jupiter Return, which was exact January 9.

- Obama's Lunar Return that includes the date of the inauguration started on January 7, 2009. The Moon returned to her natal position at 13.40 UT so the Lunar Return horoscope is cast for that moment.
- Obama's natal Jupiter is 00.52 Aquarius.
- In the Lunar Return chart, we find Jupiter at 00.33 Aquarius, conjunct the Midheaven (career, status, recognition, authority) 02.34 Aquarius.
- On the exact day of the inauguration, the Sun was conjunct Mercury at just under 1 degree of Aquarius, and both were therefore exactly conjunct Obama's Jupiter.

The lunar chorus is loud and strong. A stunning backdrop of a series of five consecutive lunations from January 11 through March 11, including two Eclipses, all lined up with natal positions. This picture in itself indicates intensity, and a major life event unfolding during those two months (this series is outlined in detail on page 129).

Both Queen Elizabeth II and Obama's Lunar Return charts for these life events are textbook Lunar Return examples. Both demonstrate the point that other very clear and symbolically appropriate astrology is at work and, in this respect, we don't *need* the Lunar Return chart to arrive at the correct interpretations/predictions. The purpose of the Lunar Return is to confirm and amplify the message for any particular month, which is why you only need to locate the key features rather than concerning yourself with the whole chart.

Lunar Returns are another string to the astrologer's bow. They can teach us a great deal about zooming in on relevant symbolism, and they add to the intriguing purpose of the Moon as the celestial chorus, in both her symbolism and her timing.

Resources and Further Reading

For Chapter 1 Moon Signs, you will need to know your natal Moon. To look this up, go to astrotheme.com. You will need to know the date, place, and time of your birth. If you do not know the time of birth, then simply enter 12:00 midday. This will produce what is known as a Noon Chart—note, however, that this chart will not be wholly accurate in terms of the Ascendant and the position of the Moon.

For Chapter 2 Moon Watching, you will need to know which sign the Moon is in for any given day. You can also find this information at astrotheme.com.

For Chapter 3 Lunations and Eclipses, go to mooncalendar.astro-seek.com to look up all the lunations (New and Full Moons) and Eclipses in a given year. The tables cover from 1900 to 2035.

Ephemerides

These are tables that list the motion of the planets for every single day and which also shows the date, sign, and degree of New and Full Moons, and the dates for when these are Eclipses. The tables are laid out in columns, one for each of the planets.

Each day starts at midnight (a 0h Ephemerides) or at midday (a Noon Ephemerides). I personally always use a 0h Ephemerides as it can be confusing working across two days instead of just looking at one 24-hour period.

Consulting your Ephemerides enables you to plan your way ahead or to look at the journeys you have already made. You can find where any planet was/is/will be at any given time.

You can buy the books (there are many to choose from) and, depending on how far back/forward you want to explore, you can choose Ephemerides that cover this century and also the last. Alternatively, you can find the information online. Here are a few recommendations.

Books

The Ephemeris, 2001–2060, Jupiter Press
The New International Ephemerides, 1900–2050, Aureus Press

Online

Astrodienst: astro.com/swisseph/swepha_e.htm
Cafe Astrology: cafeastrology.com/ephemeris.html

Software

Astrogold: https://apps.apple.com/fr/app/astro-gold/id430270438

Essential Astrology

If you like this book, you might also enjoy my other astrology book, *Essential Astrology* (ISBN 971800652354), published by CICO Books. This informative guide contains a detailed exploration of the Sun signs and also looks at the influence of all the other planetary positions in your birth chart.

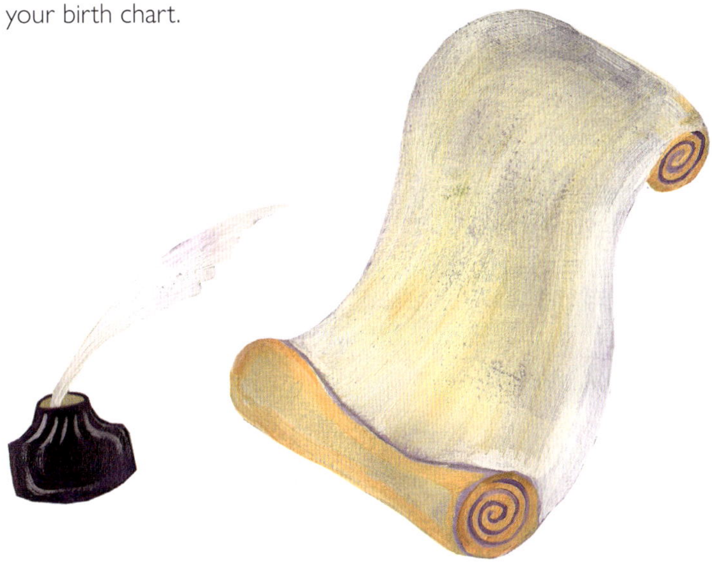

Index

Acknowledgments

My heartfelt gratitude to my long-time friend, colleague, and fellow author Elisabeth Brooke, who was the biggest source of support and guidance throughout the writing of this book. There were many delays and changes, but Elisabeth read every single word of this text before it went to print, made countless invaluable suggestions at both an editorial and subject material level, and kept me attached to a lifeline of encouragement and constructive feedback.

This book would not be complete without acknowledging my very first tutors. To Maggie Hyde, who still somehow manages to sit on my shoulder every time I write, and in grateful memory of the irreplaceable Geoffrey Cornelius, who opened my eyes to this other world.

Picture Credits

Illustrations by Eleanor Carter © CICO Books, apart from the following:

Sarah Perkins © CICO Books: pp12-13, p15, p16, p17, p20, p21, p23, p25 (symbols)

© Adobe Stock and the following creators:
Peter ananaline: p19; BYAI: p11, p27, p69, p109, p131; dartlab: p11, p27, p69, p109, p131; Hermes Furian: p111, p117, p119, p123; Назарій: p2, pp6-7, pp8-9, pp12-13, p32, p35, p38, p41, p44, p47, p50, p53, p56, p59, p62, p65, p70, p72, p75, p78, p81, p84, p87, p90, p93, p96, p99, p102, p105; Studio_3321: p2, p6, p8, p12, p41, p70, p81